REGAINING

STRENGTH

A COLLECTION OF INSPIRATIONAL PASSAGES FROM
THE REAL LIFE
EVENTS OF ONE CHRISTIAN WOMAN

BY:

JANICE MCDONALD

ARTICLES EDITED BY LISA MATHEWS

But those who hope in the
Lord will renew their Strength.
Isaiah 40:31 (NLT)

Women Regaining Strength

Publishing Company, LLC ©2009
P O Box 11583
Wilmington, Delaware 19850
www.wrspublishing.com
www.womenregainingstrength.com

Today is January 17, 2009 and my computer froze. After shutting it down completely and rebooting, I noticed that I had lost a significant amount of data.

Normally, I would be in a panic at such devastating news, but thank God seventeen days earlier on December 31, 2008, I decided to back up my files.

While restoring the data, I came across a file that read "Book Regaining Strength." Immediately I laughed and paused asking myself, "what happened to your quest to complete this book?" I was reminded of how I had endeavored to finish it seven months earlier, but delays and other obligations got in the way.

For a moment I thought, "another failed attempt at completing a task, time, money and effort wasted." But then I noticed that the task was nearly complete. Hmmm, maybe the delay was good I thought.

Maybe this book was set to be released at such a time as this when the hope and faith of many people are dashed from a failing economy, job loss, dissolution of companies and organizations in business for decades, crime rates rising, and reports of new depression cases climbing.

Maybe one person will find themselves in need of an encouraging word that will enable them to place their confidence in a God who cannot fail and will restore all that was lost.

My prayer is that someone will find what they need in this compilation of short stories and become challenged to pick-up the pieces of a shattered life or broken heart, and move confidently toward Regaining Strength.

Women Regaining Strength a Christian ministry dedicated to encouraging, strengthening and building confidence was launched on January 4, 2007. In faith and at the prompting of the Holy Spirit, Janice McDonald moved to create a Web site featuring inspirational articles to share the gospel of Jesus Christ.

Through this avenue, Janice hopes to inspire other women and men to seek a personal relationship with Christ. In staying strong in the Lord and the Power of His Might, and placing their hopes in God, He will renew their strength.

This book was created after one of Janice's colleagues asked whether WRS would eventually become a magazine. She had printed out an article for a friend, who really found it helpful. Janice decided to compile her 2007 and 2008 Web site issues into a book. She hopes it will bless those of the faithful without computers, and others who might enjoy the articles in a traditional book format.

ACKNOWLEDGEMENTS

Without God's help, this book—and WRS itself-- would not have been possible. To our Lord and Savior Jesus Christ be all the Glory and Honor forever. I thank the Lord for His gentle guidance and correction. His Word says that our gifts will make room for us. I would not have known of my gift and love for writing until He showed me the path. I can accomplish all things through Jesus Christ, Who strengthens me.

To my husband, Vaughn McDonald: Thanks for allowing me to take on yet another endeavor. I know at times I get on all your nerves, ever changing. I love you and thank God for your patience.

To my mother, Elder Jane Coppedge: I thank God for your continual support. You never stutter in your confidence in the Christ in me. You listen and encourage each of my endeavors. I've inherited your determination and drive. You're a true inspiration and I thank God for blessing me with the Greatest Mom. I love you.

To my father, Jesse Coppedge: Like Mom, thanks for being there, for being such a strong support, and for passing out all those business cards. You've been the best father! I love you. J & J Floor Care - (302) 354-3793

To my children, William and Vaughn: I know you get tired of all the time I spend hogging the computer at times-- thanks for getting off of it for me! I love you both, and I'm very, very proud of you.

My sisters, Cherri Carr; Sandy Hughes; Mariama Scott and Tahira: I love you all. Cherri and Sandy, thanks for looking forward to the WRS articles every month, and never ceasing to encourage me.

My brother, Steve Lockhart: Thank you so much for your support down there in Tennessee—I love you, Big Brother!

To my brother, Richard Tilden: You're never forgotten, and we all miss your goofy laugh.

To my pastor, Reverend Aaron R. Moore: Your famous words: "Your misery will one day be your ministry." I thank God for your support and instruction to do everything in a Spirit of Excellence to the Glory and Honor of God. I love you.

Lisa Mathews, where shall I begin? I remember sending my first article to you through the essay editing company. Your editing skills are superb, and you've always met every deadline, despite all you have to do. I am grateful to God for sending you my way, and answering my prayer that day to send my essay to the right person. He did that, and more.

Diana Martin: My sister in the Lord, for whom I thank God. You've been a great support, confidante and friend. Now you know why you had to stop by CCHS. Love you and Turquoise. Martin Travels – www.martintravels.com

To Tana Jackson thanks so much for your friendship and encouragement lady, my other sister in the Lord. I thank God for you.

To Nana: Lillian McDonald, we love you -- and thanks for all the little goodies you send all the time.

To my in-laws, Wayne and Barbara McDonald: Thank you for all your help. Mom Helen and Pop Gerstein: Keep up the excellent work in photography and video recording—Two Mules Production. I love you all.

Sam Davis: I know you don't like being called out, but oh well. You're my inspiration, lady—love you!

To Manna Christian Fellowship Church: Thanks for all your support and encouragement. I thank God for you all, and especially our Mothers of the church. I love you all, and now you don't need a computer to read the articles!

Julio Cardenas, my other big brother in the Lord: In my brother's absence, I thank God for you. You're always there to encourage and help everyone behind the scene, what a beautiful spirit—love you!

Dr. Milton Harris and Brooksi: Thanks for all the great times we shared with the piano playing – I love you guys. To Dr. Harris – thank you for your wonderful teaching. You're the maestro!

Steve Ward, "The Piano Man," and another big brother of mine. You remind me so much of my brother Stevie, and your birthdays are two days apart. Thanks for sharing your talents with me. And thanks, Lisa—love you guys! www.5linx.net/steveward/.

Bayo Gbadebo, "Mr. Business Man": Thanks for jumping on board to become one of WRS's monthly writers, and for sharing all your wisdom. NuTax Financial Services www.nutax.com.

Anelda Ballard: Thank you, Minister Ballard, for your anointed writings every month. We connected right away. I love you. Jazzy Kitty Marketing & Publishing Co. www.jazzykittygreetings.biz.

Courtney Gale, "Mr. Computer Man": I can always come to you with any computer questions, and you have an answer immediately. Thank you so much, guy! Urban Headlines Magazine www.urbanheadlines.com.

Lisa Williams (La La) Jackie Henderson, and Angie Collazo, my colleagues at work, thanks for all your support. Lisa, thanks for the encouragement and great food. Jackie, thanks for never ceasing to encourage me about the articles, lady. I appreciate it—and I'm glad you enjoy them!

David Mudie, www.effectivelyspeaking.com, thanks for all the free articles on speaking and your tools to overcoming fear.

Chaplain Marva, Darren McNeil, Minister Lolley, Tom Hayman, Vonnie and Larry, Kelley and Rachel, Donna, Trina, Debbie (Manna – thanks for the very 1st donation lady, before I even asked – I won't forget it),and Joanne – thank you all for your friendship support and encouragement.

Terrell Scott, thanks so much for the software it was a huge blessing. Your are most kind and generous, may God bless you.

Faith Community Partnership (FCP), Renee Beaman, Kenneth Hilton, Kevin Coleman, Joyce Bunkley, Angela Crump, Pearl Livingston, Darryl Simms, James and Denise Harrison, Jane Coppedge and Sister Harriett—thank you guys for spreading the awareness of HIV/AIDS.

Tom Hayman, Art, Onna, Minister Lolley, Pastor Blount, Bishop Nyansera, Evangelist White, www.gloryunlimited.com, Donna, Shabach Productions, Trina and all the WRS faithful readers I thank you for welcoming Women Regaining Strength Christian Magazine in your hearts and computers. Your support helped to make this all possible and I am eternally grateful to you all!

CONTENTS

Positioned For Transition

It's another beautiful Sunday afternoon, and my spirit just finished feeding on the Word of God spoken at our 10:00 a.m. worship service.

After sharing greetings, news, and laughter with family members and my sisters and brothers in the Lord in the sanctuary, I gather my younger son who is playing tag on the church steps with friends in his Sunday clothing, and instruct my eldest son to end his intense conversation with friends and we head on our journey home.

As soon as we reach the house, I rush up to my room, and immediately change from my Sunday best to lounge pants, a t-shirt, and slippers. On my way downstairs, I give my younger son a little scolding--Is your room straight? Are your clothes ready?—and make sure he's prepared for school the next day before he goes outside to play. Then I run through that evening's dinner menu in my mind, double-checking that I have all the ingredients on hand. Finally, I grab my favorite blanket and head to the living room. I flip through the channels in search of my favorite kind of show: an animal documentary.

My love for this type of program undoubtedly stems from my youth, when our whole family gathered around the TV at 7 p.m. sharp, to watch Mutual of Omaha's Wild Kingdom. Back then, we didn't have specialized children's channels, like Nickelodeon, the Cartoon Network, or the Disney Channel. A child wasn't able to choose what he or she wanted to watch from several different TV's. We had to watch whatever our parents were watching.

When our family returned home from church on Sundays, my mother would watch Channel 28 – a gospel station. Then, around 7:00 p.m., came the big treat: we'd get to watch Wild Kingdom. I can still hear the theme music playing in my ears, along with the distinctive drone of the narrator's voice. We kids sat, glued to the set, as the chirping of crickets began in the background, and the tall grass rustled as exotic animals ventured through the African Plains to reach their destinations.

My favorite animal was the Lion. I was fascinated by that magnificent creature's beautiful mane, a fitting adornment which was also a dead giveaway when trying to sneak up on prey. And his powerful roar let everyone know he was King of the Jungle.

Then there was the Lioness with her agility and prowess, who after doing all the work in the hunt, steps aside so the King can eat first. Today, as a grown-up, I have to laugh, because I'd probably say, "Now hold up there just one minute, King, you did nothing to bring this food into the house. You were out in the jungle all day, roaring and parading around while *I* slaved over this meal. And furthermore, Mr. Big Shot, the kids need to eat first!" After a bit of this fussing, though, I'm sure I'd let him eat. But I have to admit, I'm intrigued by the unity displayed by every member of the pride. The lions know that they need the cooperation of every member during a hunt to ensure that they all will eat. Without such unity, they could die.

No matter how many times I've seen these animal documentaries, I still get great enjoyment from them. Today, I'm watching a starving crocodile as he sits in wait on the mighty Mara River. Though it's been a very long time since he's eaten—crocodiles are equipped to survive a whole year without food--he doesn't dare move. He knows that, at any moment now, scores of wildebeest on their annual migration will surely cross the river, ending his forced fast.

Through the torturous, heat-soaring days--which often turn into months--without food, with nagging insects toiling to penetrate his leathery flesh, he never relinquishes his position in the crocodile-packed river.

Steadfastly and patiently he waits, his powerful jaws capable of 3000 pounds of force opened ever so gently. In lean days he exerts only the necessary energy for survival until he receives his reward. He is positioned for transition – and finally he does transcend, into a bounty of flesh from the unsuspecting wildebeest who meets his untimely demise in the crocodile's massive jaws.

And so it is that we, too, need to be just as determined as the crocodile in positioning ourselves for reward. We must remain unyielding in the many stormy and sun-beaten days to come, the long and difficult times that threaten to keep us from transcending into our God Ordained destinies.

We must not be moved by discouraging comments, failed ventures, nor lost opportunities. Such dispiriting events threaten to penetrate our faith barriers, dampen our spirits, and bring about doubt and uncertainty that our plans will ever work, or that God's promises for our lives will be fulfilled.

We must not grow weary in well doing, for at the proper time we will reap a harvest if we do not give up (Galatians 6:19). For God is not a man, that He should lie, nor a son of man, that He should change His mind. Does He speak and then not act? Does He promise and not fulfill (Numbers 23:19)? No, God does not. All things shall come to pass – everything that God has promised us.

But before the fulfillment of His Promise, there is work that we must do. There is a level of preparedness or placement we must reach in our businesses, ministries, families, jobs, schooling, faith, diligence, prayer, and worship. We must ready ourselves for God to transcend us at His appointed time, and lead us into the bounty of reward prepared for His ultimate glory.

We must become—and remain--Positioned for Transition.

THE FOUR CHILDREN

It was March 8, 2008, and the day was gray and gloomy. The rain seemed to pour down in buckets at times, relentlessly reminding us of its power to flood our surroundings in a matter of minutes.

Now, as I sat in the large church beside my sister Cherri, I listened to the rain falling soft like a warm shower as it hit the glass windows. The lights were dim, and the old wood of the pews and wall paneling seemed dull. I was reminded of the church of my youth, Revival Fellowship, under the direction of the late and great Pastor Pearlie Mae Young. I only needed to hear the guitar, a rarity in most churches nowadays, to start playing and someone to sing an old tune like "I'm Running for My Life," and it would be as if I were truly there once more.

The church was full to capacity, with people standing along the side walls. At the front, a video played, showing photos of the deceased. A collage with more photos of the departed and his loved ones was on display in a two foot-tall frame near the altar.

Cherri and I took our seats to the left of the church in the middle section, the area designated for "friends" of the deceased. As we waited for the program to start, my sister leaned over and whispered, "Don't act up now, Janice. There's a man in the back videotaping the entire service, and we don't want you caught on tape for everyone to see." We both smiled, lightening the intense mood a bit.

"Do you think we should we go up and view the body?" I asked. "Yes," my sister answered, with some reluctance. "We need to let Mom know we are here."

We made our way to where my mother and stepfather sat with my aunts and uncle, five rows behind the immediate family. After greeting them and giving Mom a kiss, Cherri and I approached the front of the church.

Red carnations, along with more flowers in yellow and white, adorned the beautiful gray and silver casket, which appeared lined with fine white cotton. Inside lay a gray-headed gentleman, his skin browned and wrinkled with age. According to usual custom in the placement of the deceased, his arms were folded. He wore a black suit, white shirt, and tie. This man was my grandfather, whom I had never really known.

He looked much different than he had when Cherri and I had last seen him, very briefly, at the Repass following the funeral of my eldest brother. He was much heavier then, before he became ill, I noted to myself as we walked back to our seats.

During the service I learned that my grandfather had been in a nursing home, ironically one owned by the same hospital at which I worked. I thought, *If I had known him, maybe I could have visited him.* Then I remembered the day I had recognized him at the hospital, and how I had greeted him with a smile, hoping he would recall that I was his granddaughter. He mumbled, "Hi," his head bowed as if he wanted nothing more to do with me. Sadly, I watched him walk past me into the hospital lobby as I held the door, never really acknowledging me.

I thought about my father, who had been killed when I was six months old, and his mother. I remembered how my sisters and brother had found our way to her doorstep one day when we were little. We walked for what seemed like miles to our little feet, and knocked on the door. A woman opened it only slightly, and stood in the darkness behind it, never revealing her face. "We're your grandkids!" we announced, expecting that this revelation would cause her to fling open the door with excitement, embrace us, and invite us in to show us pictures of our deceased father, her only child. Instead, she replied, "Oh," and quietly shut the door.

My siblings and I had stood there on the steps for a few minutes, hoping that maybe she was unhooking a chain to the door. Surely she wanted to know us, we'd thought. We were her only grandchildren. But the door never reopened. My siblings and I walked home silently, hurt and shocked at the reception we had received. We never mentioned that painful incident again.

I quickly snapped back to reality in the church, reminding myself that I could do nothing for the departed, for they had wanted nothing to do with me.

My younger sister Sandy arrived and sat in the back of the church, while the mourners were still filing by the body to pay their last respects. I greeted her and asked whether she wanted to move up closer with us, but she said she was fine right there. I'm sure my sister felt as out of place and unwanted as Cherri and I did. Nonetheless, we knew it was good that we had come to support our mother, aunts and uncle.

My mother and her own three siblings had longed for a relationship with the father who had deserted them in their youth. Their mother--my grandmother—had died when they were young. It seemed as if Life had hit them with some pretty heavy blows.

The four children were sent to different foster homes, and many years would go by before they would find and reconcile with their father. Despite great efforts on their parts, they never managed to achieve a true bond with him. Shortly after he abandoned their mother, he had started a new life that included a wife and seven more children, one of them a stepdaughter. There was no room left for my mother and her siblings.

I sat now at the funeral, listening to all the accolades of this great man. I listened to stories of his faithfulness to family, church and, most of all, Jesus. I was thankful for the one legacy he left us: the desire to cherish and serve the Lord. I'm sure he had silently prayed for his eldest four children to come to know our Lord and Savior Jesus Christ.

One by one, the speakers at the front of the church mentioned my grandfather's seven children and his wife of 56 years. "No!" I wanted to scream. "There are *eleven* children, not seven!" But I stayed quiet. This was neither the time nor place for such an outburst.

The service continued, and with each passing moment slipped the hope that someone—anyone-- would mention those four children.

Then a speaker began to read the cards and resolutions which had been sent to comfort the family. I was elated when they acknowledged a letter written by my pastor, who had come to support us, along with other congregants of our church. Perhaps now the four children would be acknowledged, I thought. But that letter was never read.

Another letter from our city councilman, however, somehow managed to slip through the cracks of scrutiny. The speaker seemed to choke on her words as she read the name of the addressee at the end: Elder Jane Coppedge, my mother and one of the four children. A heavy silence covered the sanctuary, as if a great injustice had just been unveiled. It seemed to last for an eternity.

The program overseer stepped up and asked all clergy to come to the pulpit. He invited our surprised pastor to sing a solo and read a scripture. In the atmosphere of discontent and confusion, I wondered what he'd say. Then I reminded myself that it wasn't his place to say anything. Wisely, he did exactly what was asked of him, and delivered an inspiring solo.

As the service continued, one of the seven children at the front of the church who had been sharing fond memories of his father called out, "Will all seven of my father's children please stand?" I watched in both horror and pride, as my elderly aunt, who was still recovering from a lengthy illness, rose to her feet, her daughters beside her in support. She stood as if to say, "I'm one of the four you keep forgetting to mention. I'm my father's first child." She held her position until everyone saw her standing along with the seven children, then quietly sat down. My other aunt, uncle, and mother sat humbly. I knew it was taking every bit of strength and dignity they had not to lash out. I decided to follow their lead, and remain silent.

I looked over at them often, especially my mother, who wasn't feeling well, to see if I could read their emotions. But they never flinched.

Some people began to whisper, *Why are there eleven children listed in the program? Where are the other four?* "Silenced," I told myself.

I felt the hurt and pain that my mother and her sisters and brother declined to show, and at one point during the funeral I had to excuse myself. I headed to the ladies' room to regroup, where I shed a few tears and prayed, asking God to help me avoid unleashing my anger.

After my emotions had subsided somewhat and I returned to my seat for the Eulogy, I asked myself, what about those four children? The youngest, my mother, was now 63 years old. Would the rest of their father's family continue to pretend that they didn't exist? Who would acknowledge the four children as they sat silently in their seats, like a faded portrait of my grandfather's past life, their heads held up in pride?

I wondered how they could remain so dignified, no doubt hoping all the while that just one person would make them feel welcome. Who would say how proud they were of these four children as they came to pay their last respects to a father who had never seemed to want them?

Who would notice their grace in forgiveness and reconciliation, as they refused to show the pain of never truly knowing the great man referenced by speaker after speaker at the podium?

Who would remind these four that they were neither flukes, nor mistakes? Who would honor the strength they exhibited as they sat through the entire two-and-a-half-hour funeral, their existence acknowledged only once, during the reading of the obituary? Who would remember their sad smiles as they walked last behind their father's casket, although they should have been first? Who would tell them that, though they had been sent from home to home, abused, neglected, abandoned, and alone, there was always a plan for them?

And then, as the rain fell hard outside the old church, Jesus reminded me of His Word, (Isaiah 44:21): *I have created you. You will not be forgotten by Me!* He reassured me, I will speak of them for they kept my commandment *(Exodus 20:12) "Honor your father and mother." Then you will live a long, full life.* And He comforted me with His promise, (Hebrews 13:5): *"I will never leave you nor forsake you."*

God would acknowledge The Four Children.

To Elder Jane (Janie) Coppedge (Mom), Charles Richard Thomas (Uncle Dicky), Sylvia Kee (Aunt Chubby), and Mary Ann Davis (Aunt Mary): Thank you for honoring your father; we admire your love, forgiving spirit, humility and bravery.

And for anyone who has ever been abandoned, rejected, disowned, hurt, or abused, Jesus reminds us that He wants all of His children.

Regaining Strength

It was the big day: the Fourth Grade Talent Show. I was up next, and my heart seemed ready to explode in my chest from anticipation. *You're up next, Janice,* I told myself, *"It's too late to quit now."* I nervously adjusted my white top, black pants and hat – the make-shift outfit I had pulled together for my dance number.

My best friend and I had spent weeks tirelessly rehearsing a hip hop routine choreographed to "Don't Stop Till You Get Enough," one of my favorite songs. I loved Michael Jackson's songs, listening and dancing to them in my bedroom for hours on end.

As I waited backstage, I recalled how a two-person dance performance had suddenly become a one-girl show. I missed my best friend, who had refused to perform with me after a heated argument just a few weeks earlier.

I quenched my desire to bolt off stage as the music began, and tried not to think about the huge auditorium packed with classmates and teachers. "Go Janice, go Janice!" I heard the crowd cheer, boosting my self-confidence and inspiring me to dance my best. As I took a final bow and walked off the stage, I felt a true sense of pride. Another, less confident fourth-grader might have canceled her performance, but I had courageously pulled it off alone.

Now, twenty-one years later, I marvel at the strength and bravery I displayed that day. I wonder where they vanished to as I stand before the mirror, taking in the image of the pounds withered from my body and the bags beneath my eyes. Sleepless nights, brought on by the double stresses of a failing marriage and financial ruin, have taken their toll on me.

Had I lost my childish faith and hope after that fateful talent show, when the first, second, and third place winners were announced –and my name was not among them? I remember that crushing moment as if it were yesterday, and how I cried inconsolably. What I wouldn't give now to have my fourth grade strength and innocence once again to soar above this pain.

But I'm older now, and the days when my biggest worry was a talent show dance number are long gone. Surely, I can't allow worry and disappointment to dominate every facet of my life, slowly and silently killing me.

You know God's word, I encourage myself: *Who of you by worrying can add a single hour to his life* (Matthew 6:27*)? Do not be anxious about anything, but in everything, by prayer and petition, with thanksgiving, present your requests to God* (Philippians 4:6). But as hard as I try not to be, I find myself exceedingly anxious for the pain of betrayal to end.

I can't give up on life now, I tell myself, no matter how troubling the circumstances. I would need to draw from a greater strength than my own: *I will live and not die and declare the works of the Lord* (Psalms 118:17). With a new resolve in spirit, I clean my face, reapply my make-up, pin my clothes that no longer fit my frail-looking body, and begin to pick up the pieces of my life.

I envision myself in brighter days ahead. I lay my hands on my stomach and begin to pray, speaking restoration to all that was lost in the storm of betrayal, my appetite and self-confidence. I begin to worship, praise, and dance beyond my present condition.

Soon, I tap into a strength measured by neither muscle mass nor the ability to endure the toughest circumstances. I draw from the strength of family: the mother, father, sister, brother, Pastor and friends who prayed, encouraged, and uplifted me. Most of all, I tap into Jesus: *Be strong in the Lord and the power of His might* (Ephesians 6:10).

I tell Jesus again that I love Him and then, gazing into my mirror, I say, "I love you, too, Janice. You're going to make it."

Finally, I am regaining strength.

TAKE CARE OF YOURSELF

If you don't take care of yourself, then who will?

This is a familiar phrase that I have found to be very true.

From birth, we females seem to possess an overwhelming nurturing attribute: the need, willingness and desire to take care of someone or something.

As young girls, most of us played with our Barbie® dolls, Easy-Bake Ovens and dollhouses, further developing this attribute. In adulthood, we women dream of beautiful, romantic weddings, try to keep our houses spotless, and experiment with different recipes and menus to rival the world's greatest chef. In essence, we strive to become Martha Stewart clones!

We place our careers, a "must-have" new dress, or a long-anticipated trip to the hairstylist on hold to ensure the prosperity of our families. We are the most likely of the two genders to sacrifice both our long-term and everyday desires and place the needs of others before our own.

By all indications, we are living as "Virtuous Women," and it is good:

Proverbs 31:24-31 - She makes linen garments and sells them, and supplies the merchants with sashes. She is clothed with strength and dignity; she can laugh at the days to come. She speaks with wisdom, and faithful instruction is on her tongue. She watches over the affairs of her household and does not eat the bread of idleness. Her children arise and call her blessed; her husband also, and he praises her: "Many women do noble things, but you surpass them all." Charm is deceptive, and beauty is fleeting; but a woman who fears the Lord is to be praised. Give her the reward she has earned, and let her works bring her praise at the city gate.

Yet despite all this fitting praise, we virtuous women suffer one disadvantage: Sometimes we equate taking a break to care for ourselves as a selfish-- instead of selfless—act. But the truth is, we must first take care of ourselves-- spiritually, emotionally, mentally and physically—in order to effectively take care of others.

During a sermon one Sunday, my pastor referenced the safety demonstration given on airplanes just before take-off: The flight attendant instructs passengers on the correct use of oxygen masks, should they be activated during a flight. Adult passengers with small children are told to place the oxygen masks over their own faces before their children's.

I remember being a bit taken back when I heard those instructions on my first flight. At first, I did not understand the concept of securing my own life before the lives of my children, who were two and nine at the time. As the flight attendant continued her speech, however, I soon realized that, in placing the mask over myself first, I ensured that I would remain conscious, and therefore able to place the oxygen masks on my children.

And so it is with life: We women have to take care of ourselves to ensure that we will be able to help take care of someone else. That someone may be a child, a husband, a mother, father, sister, brother, or friend. It could also be someone who needs to see Jesus lifting your spirit to bring you through a particular circumstance or trial-- or someone who simply needs an encouraging word.

Today is January 27, 2007, and a few hours before I wrote these words, I received some crushing news. I immediately felt as if I needed a hiatus, that I should be on a secluded island somewhere, far away from everything and everybody.

I threw myself a real pity party, and then began to pray. I waited for God to tell me that He would devour my enemies, those who had wronged me. Instead, He said, "Janice, you're not trusting Me." After a moment or two, I realized that His assessment of my behavior was correct. So, I decided to take a break and do something special for myself. I finished pressing my hair, put on my clothes, and took myself out to dinner.

As I sat at a table in one of my favorite restaurants, alone--feeling the glances of my fellow diners as I began to eat my steak--I began to finish this article for my newsletter. The disappointment from earlier in the day only served to intensify my creative spirit, adding further validation to the title "Take Care of Yourself."

After an enjoyable meal, I decided to see an uplifting movie, too. I chose "The Pursuit of Happyness," which perfectly fit the bill. The entire evening was refreshing, and I was glad that God had ended my pity party.

I encourage you all to take a break for yourselves, and indulge in a bubble bath surrounded with candles. Put on your favorite nightgown, and try a new way of doing your hair and make-up. Send the kids off to school one morning and take the day off from work. Dub that day your "Me Day" and head to the mall for window shopping, or pick up that DVD from the video store that only you want to see. Get a manicure, or head to the spa. Buy yourself a dozen roses. Join a gym or buy a new exercise video. And last but not least, attend a church service, and join in fellowship with others. Receive the Word of God, which will strengthen your spirit and carry you through both good and troubling times.

Take care of yourself – so you can take care of others!

Forgive And Remember Differently

Forgive. What a challenging word for us all when we preach a familiar quote: *"What goes around, comes around."*

If truth be told, most of us are sometimes guilty of wanting to see the hurt, pain, and humiliation bestowed upon us by an offender returned to them, one hundred fold. In the past I myself have rationalized, Well, God's Word says: *Be not deceived; God is not mocked: for whatsoever a man soweth, that shall he also reap (Galatians 6:7).* God's Word is clearly true, for people reap both good and bad from their actions. But did God mean for us to wait, expecting--even longing--to see the harvest of our offender's rotten crops? No, He didn't, for His Word also says: *And be kind to one another, tender-hearted, forgiving each other, just as God in Christ also has forgiven you (Ephesians 4:32).* Real forgiveness does not long to see The Big Payback. Forgiveness allows God to judge, and either pardon or punish as He sees fit. God is Sovereign, and He will do whatever He chooses.

One day during a service, I went up for prayer, seeking strength and encouraging words from the Lord that would carry me through a tough situation. Instead of the uplifting words I expected, however, I received a rebuke from the Lord. The minister told me, "God said that you must forgive." Immediately I became defensive, thinking, Forgive? Ha! What do you think I've been doing all this time? Then the minister went on, "God said that when you forgive, He will supply the deliverance you need." At that point, I threw up my hands in frustration and thought, What else am I supposed to do? Haven't I been forgiving all along?

I went home and looked up the definition of "forgive" in my Bible. Directly beside the word was the simple definition: *to pardon, excuse, or offer forgiveness.*

I suddenly realized that I had a whole list of people whom I hadn't truly forgiven. I hadn't released them from The Big Payback-- or from ever returning to say to me, "I'm so sorry. Please forgive me for all the hurt and pain I caused you."

The Word of God rang in my ears: *But if you do not forgive men their sins, your Father will not forgive your sins (Mathew 6:15).* I truly wanted God to forgive me for my own transgressions, so I tried even harder to move toward forgiving those who had hurt me.

By coincidence a few days later, I received an e-mail from a friend that contained this quote from Henry Ward Beecher: *"I can forgive, but I cannot forget" is only another way of saying, ''I cannot forgive.''*

My first reaction was, "Forget? They can't mean that *literally!"* My friends often joke that my memory is like an elephant's. I just couldn't help feeling that there were some things I didn't *want* to forgive and forget. Was that so wrong?

But Henry Ward Beecher wasn't finished. The quote went on: *Forgiveness ought to be like a canceled note -- torn in two, and burned up, so that it never can be shown against one.* The words were very clear: Forgiveness should never be used as an I.O.U., with the offense thrown back at the offender by the offendee, and used against him. I decided to make a new quote, one that I felt was more fitting: *Forgive and remember differently!*

The truth is, there are some experiences in my life that I choose never to forget. They have helped to forge the person I am today, and shown me God's sustaining power, strength, and grace. They have brought to life for me His Word: *No weapon formed against me shall prosper (Isaiah 54:17), but those who hope in the Lord will renew their strength. They will soar on wings like eagles; they will run and not grow weary, they will walk and not be faint (Isaiah 40:31), if God is for us who can be against us? (Romans 8:31).*

I choose not to forget these things so that I will never cease to give God glory for all He has done for me. That way, I will always have my testimony to share with others of how God brought me through some tough spots, and how He will do the same for them. Instead of forgetting, I will simply remember differently.

I make a conscious effort not to remember certain events in ways that hold bitterness or anger, or seek to receive repayment. I decided to forgive and remember differently—remember Godly--even the most hurtful things, for *in all things God works for the good of those who love Him, who have been called according to His purpose (Romans 8:28)*. These painful events continually refine, prune, and expose my true self; challenging me to strive toward a more Godly character.

There are a few difficult instances in particular from my life that I choose to forgive and remember differently. For example:

My Molestation As a Child - Instead of crying as I think of the violation of my innocence, I remember a Bible study that challenged me to forgive my offender. I remember an individual, sorry and truly repentant of his sins, and the prayer he sent up to God to show him His grace and mercy. That's what the man told me when I wrote him a simple letter five years ago, saying I forgave him and that he was no longer obligated to me. He died recently, and I'm happy that God challenged me that night to forgive.

The Layoff From My Job When I Was Five Months Pregnant—My employer's intention was to fire me, but they had no legal basis for that action. Instead, they suddenly gave me a pink slip and sent me home one day. I don't remember the months of torment and harassment leading up to the layoff. Instead, I remember all the doctor appointments I was able to attend for my high risk pregnancy, without having to request time off from work. I remember the rest and peace I enjoyed for four months before the birth of my second child, and my return to work on a part-time basis while he was still young. I would never have been able to accomplish these things if I hadn't been laid off.

The Two Sparsely-attended Ministries I Oversaw At Church – It was somewhat discouraging at times when not many people could make it to the classes I taught, one a small sewing class, and the other teaching Biblical and life lessons to young ladies. But the discouragement always turned to joy when I saw the enthusiasm of an individual whom I was able to help. I'll remember that God saw this faithfulness, and that neither time nor words were wasted in those ministries. Although I couldn't see His purpose at the time, He knew that the groundwork was being set for greater things.

God is challenging us all to Forgive and Remember Differently – remember "Godly" and give Him the glory!

TRIUMPHANT OVER FEAR

Has God given us over to a spirit of fear?

No, I do not believe the Lord has made us fearful, for His Word clearly states: *God has not given us a spirit of fear; but of power and love and of a sound mind (2 Timothy 1:7).*

So if God didn't bring us fear, then who did? Well, we can't always blame everything on the Devil. For some of us, an often overwhelming, general sense of fear may have been brought on by a traumatic life experience. Others of us may develop personal fears of particular things or situations that make us feel uncomfortable.

We all have the power through Jesus Christ to become triumphant, but at times we may find ourselves shrinking back in fear. Instead of waiting for God and His deliverance to help us succeed, we choose our own way of dealing with anxiety-provoking situations. And in doing so, we unfortunately end up repeating the same trials all over again— this time, with the extra baggage of fear.

But what is it that we really fear? Do we fear being viewed as a failure, being let down by others, humiliated, mocked, or even isolated? Are we afraid of being wrong, having our hopes and dreams dashed, or acquiring a greater number of responsibilities?

My own greatest fear is speaking or performing in front of an audience, a dread that was probably brought on by the fateful childhood talent show I wrote about in the Regaining Strength essay.

For years afterward, I broke out in a sweat at the thought of having to sing. Whenever I did, my voice would quiver with fright, and I needed to visit the rest room many times right before the performance. My fear virtually paralyzed me, preventing me from the enjoyment of venturing past my safety zone and trying new things.

Thank God that, nine years ago, I put in a prayer request for deliverance from this fear. Just before I was about to sing in front of a congregation, I confessed to the audience that I had a strong fear of performing in front of people, and that I believed God would one day deliver me from it: *And they have defeated him because of the blood of the Lamb and because of their testimony (Revelation 12:11).* After confessing my fear, I was able to sing that day with much more confidence. Almost everyone, no doubt, had already noticed the fear in me, and acknowledging it publicly helped me on my journey to overcoming it.

Today, when I stand before a congregation, introducing my mother as a speaker, acting as a spokeswoman for an event, or delivering a sermon, you would probably never guess the horrible grip that fear once held on me.

There were several steps I took to overcome my fear of speaking in public:

1. I confessed my fear of being in front of people and became an overcomer by the blood of the Lamb and the word of my testimony.

2. Eventually, though still fearful, I took a leap of faith and stepped forward when asked to speak or perform.

3. I began to gain confidence by practicing and polishing my speaking skills.

In August 2006, God called me to join the Ministers In Training class at my local church, Manna Christian Fellowship. At first I was a bit reluctant to accept the call as a minister—I had initially thought I wanted to sing more than preach. Years earlier, however, I had begun to acknowledge in my heart that this was indeed an area of ministering to which God was calling me. Once I accepted the idea that I would one day be a minister, I shared these thoughts with my family and close friends. At that time, I was busy ministering to my family and home, so I stayed patient until I received God's signal last summer that it was time to move into the ministry at church.

A few months later, we MITs were told that we would each be asked to speak on New Year's Eve at the Watch Night Service. My immediate reaction was a desire to shrink back in fear. I recalled how, during one of our recent MIT meetings, my voice had cracked and I had broken out in a sweat as I began to read to the group the first page of a ministry Code of Ethics I had written.

After that disaster I had told myself, "What a disappointment!" Someday, as a minister, I would have to speak in front of a whole congregation for fifteen to thirty minutes at a time. And I couldn't even make it through two minutes without starting to panic! How on earth would I ever deliver that sermon on New Year's Eve?

I recognized that I still had a problem with fear, despite my best efforts to move forward. Again, I prayed to the Lord for help. I asked for His wisdom as to how I could overcome this paralyzing fear.

In my spirit, I immediately received a response: I needed to learn and practice the skills for speaking before an audience, as had many well-known public speakers. I even remembered a story I had once heard about a Prophetess who practiced her sermons on pots and pans in her home before she began ministering.

I knew that I needed to gather some good tools to learn more about public speaking, but I didn't have the money to purchase books or tapes. So, I went to one of the best—and completely free--resources of information: the Internet. I typed in "fear of public speaking" in the search field to see if anything popped up. I was blessed to discover David Mudie's article "How to Get Over Fear of Public Speaking" on his website at www.effectivelyspeaking.com.

Mr. Mudie speaks of his former fear of public speaking, and how he worked to overcome it. He now travels the country, giving speeches and teaching seminars. I printed out all of the articles from the website, and signed up for the mailing list. I followed Mr. Mudie's tips for overcoming fear of speaking before an audience, imagining the worst things that could happen to me: being humiliated, and feeling like a failure. To my surprise and relief, when I resolved these terrifying possibilities in my spirit, I was finally able to move forward.

I went home one day after work and created a make-shift "podium" out of boxes and wrapping paper. I even crowned it with a cross I'd drawn in black magic marker.

In addition to creating my practice speaker's podium, I went into Microsoft Word on my computer and printed out pictures of different people's faces from the Clip Art photo section. I chose all kinds of faces: smiling, disgruntled, and perplexed. I added a bored-looking teenager, a crying baby, and even a couple of people who had fallen asleep – all the types of faces ministers regularly encounter in their audiences. I strung each face on one of two long ropes in a spare bedroom. At first I attached the ropes to the walls with Scotch tape, but after they fell several times, I attached one end to the door and the other to a window blind to make them stable. Then I took out my amplifier and microphone and began to practice my sermons. I recorded a few of them so that I could play them back and grow accustomed to the sound of my own voice.

I told one of my friends how I was trying to overcome my fear of public speaking, and asked if he might have some more tips for me. He encouraged me to go over to the chapel at the local hospital for which I work and practice during lunch. I was reluctant at first, as I thought the idea was a waste of time. I was probably going to be a failure anyway. And what if someone walked in while I was rehearsing? But then I realized my friend was right, and thanked him for his advice. I rehearsed at the chapel over and over, until I became comfortable speaking in a large room, which I imagined was full of people.

Finally, on that long-dreaded New Year's Eve, I approached the podium during the Watch Night Service, confident that I had done everything possible to overcome my fear. I knew that God would do the rest, and so He did. He blessed me on that day, and through all the resources he had given me: the Internet articles, the hours of practice, my supportive family and wise friend--and most of all, His answer to my prayer request.

Today, I still find myself fearful at times, about public speaking and many other life situations. But with each step I take with God, my fears continue to diminish. I still have a ways to go toward being completely fearless, but thanks to the Lord I'm on my way to becoming truly Triumphant Over Fear.

How Can We Believe?

How can I believe? That was the question I asked myself as I sat on the bed this morning, May 23, 2007. I was devastated and in tears at the news my mother had just delivered in a phone call: Yet another member of our congregation had gone home to be with the Lord.

Nadine was only 52 years of age, beautiful in both spirit and countenance. She was also blessed with what I'm sure was the voice of an angel, even though I've never actually heard one sing.

Her passing came suddenly for us all. It seemed like only yesterday that nearly every member of Manna Christian Fellowship had gathered to fast and pray for the healing of our beloved Sister in the Lord. Along with her devoted husband and beautiful daughter, a host of Nadine's family members and friends also stood as a unified testimony of faith for her healing and recovery. And as the days went by, each of us logged onto our computers to type encouraging messages onto her website and read the journal entries detailing the progress of her health.

We waited, strong in our faith and anticipating The Good News that the devastating cancer had miraculously been driven from Nadine's body. Finally, the healing that God alone could provide was revealed, but not as we had hoped. It came forth in our Sister's deliverance from a cancer-ravished body and her return home to the Lord.

Now, as I prepared for my workday, not knowing whether I could muster the strength to go in, I began to question God. "How can I believe?" I asked Him. "How can I supply the faith anymore, Lord? We all believed in You. We watched Sister Nadine as she held on, singing Your praises and rejoicing, even in the emergency room-- and then she went home to be with You. How can we continue to supply the faith when, not long ago, we watched Brother Emanuel recover after a lengthy illness? Along with our entire congregation, he danced before You in jubilation --before he, too, went home to be with You. How can we continue to believe after Little Imani bravely came to church, toting the cancer equipment attached to her frail body? When asked if she still believed God would heal her, she quickly responded, "Yes, I do!" We all believed with her until the very end--when she, too, was summoned back to Your heavenly kingdom.

So, I continued to ask of the Lord, in a hurting and childish manner, how can we bravely ignore the doctors' grim diagnoses and proclaim: "God is able!"? How can we continue to fast and pray, quoting: "Stand still and see the salvation of the Lord!"? (Exodus 14:13). How can we keep believing in Your healing powers under all of these sad and difficult circumstances?

As I drove to work, still troubled in spirit, I continued to commune with the Lord in prayer. Later that morning, I shared my feelings of doubt and frustration with my mother. She said, "Janice, we have to go on with our lives and continue to supply the faith. There are many things we will never understand about God." I knew my mom was right, but for some reason Nadine's passing had hit me especially hard.

I began to wonder about this, because many other loved ones have also gone on before me. Then I realized that Nadine's faith in healing was somehow tied in to my faith in God's delivering me, personally, from other circumstances as well. This seemed a bit selfish, as Nadine had been fighting for her very life. But as a Body of Believers, we encourage one another by viewing each other overcome difficult circumstances. I began to wonder what the purpose was in believing for those circumstances anymore.

A short time later, as I sat at my desk at work, God's Word rose up in my spirit to answer my question: Now faith is being sure of what we hope for, and certain of what we do not see. This is what the ancients were commended for. By faith we understand that the universe was formed at God's command, so that what is seen was not made out of what was visible. (Hebrews 11:1-3)

And then God reminded me of another scripture passage, this time from Hebrews 11:6: - And without faith it is impossible to please God, because anyone who comes to Him must believe that He exists and that He rewards those who earnestly seek Him. How true, I thought.

Without faith, it would be impossible to please Him – and wasn't that my earnest and sincere desire? How could I withhold the very thing He most requires of me?

I soon realized that we had all done what was required of us, and that was to supply the faith. We believe that God is able to deliver, cure, and even raise the dead – yet we must also accept that He is Sovereign; His Will shall be done. And in the cases of Sister Nadine and Brother Emanuel and Little Imani, His Will was indeed done. Although God had the infallible ability to cure each of our congregation's suffering members, He chose to bring them home with Him.

The title of the sermon God had given our pastor just this past Sunday suddenly came to my mind: "I'm All Right with It." He told us, "We must be all right with whatever God allows, and know that He is still in control of every situation." I realized that I needed to be right with God's decision today.

Will we continue to believe during the next troubling circumstance, or seeming impossibility? I asked myself. Assuredly we will, for we are a Body of Believers. The very basis of accepting Jesus Christ as our Lord and Savior is an act of faith: "Jesus is Immanuel"--which means, "God with us." (Matthew 1:23). We believe that He is God in the form of man who came to this earth to redeem us all from sin, before ascending back to heaven, and that "Salvation is found in no one else, for there is no other name under heaven given to men by which we must be saved." (Acts 4:12). God's Word is clear: There is no other way for man to be saved from sin and live a life eternal but by accepting Jesus Christ as his Lord and Savior.

Another often-quoted scripture also came to mind: "I will live and not die and declare the works of the Lord." (Psalms 118:17). Do Brother Emanuel and Sisters Nadine and Little Imani indeed live, and continue to declare God's works? The answer is yes, only now all three of them are in a heavenly place, proclaiming day and night: "Holy, holy, holy is the Lord God Almighty, who was, and is, and is to come." (Revelations 4:8). They live eternal lives through our Lord and Savior Jesus Christ (1 John 5:11), worshipping and praising God for His goodness, mercy, and grace. They declare and testify to how the Lord redeemed them, but now they do so face to face with our Savior.

The question is not "How Can We Believe?" It is "How Can we Afford Not To?"

This article is dedicated to all those who have returned home to be with the Lord – especially my brother Richard Douglas Tilden. Until the day that we shall be gathered together once again, we will miss you all-- but we rejoice that you have overcome death, and live on through our Lord and Savior Jesus Christ.

Growing up in my family, we were all small-framed—even skinny, some might say. At sixteen years of age, I weighed about 108 pounds. At eighteen, I graduated to a whopping 110 pounds, an added bonus I received a few months after giving birth to my first son.

For years, I always wanted to be an extra ten to fifteen pounds heavier, especially since females in our African-American culture are known for their voluptuous curves. I'd eat as much as I could, and that food would burn right off: cakes, fried foods, potato chips, you name it – anything and everything I thought would pack on the pounds. I even resorted to bland-tasting weight gain shakes, to no avail. I'm sure if some people had known how hard I was trying to gain weight, they would have thought I was crazy--especially if they were trying just as hard themselves to lose extra pounds.

As time went on, my body metabolism slowed and I finally kicked my nearly pack-a-day cigarette habit. It was then that I began to realize how unsatisfied I had been with myself for years.

How much time had I wasted wishing I looked older, for example? As a teenager, I applied Maybelline eyeliner and lipstick and begged my mother for pierced ears. I hoped that these outward changes would do the trick to get me into bars and nightclubs--as if that feat would be some great accomplishment. I couldn't help but remember the weekend trip getaways to Maryland with friends, or ski trips wasted arguing with my boyfriend if another woman walked by who seemed more sophisticated than I, with a few more curves in the hips. It finally dawned on me that these events were all due to my constant feelings of insecurity.

Recently, a girlfriend and I were talking over the phone about her upcoming speaking engagement. She said she couldn't help comparing her speaking skills with mine, and that she hoped she could "flow my words like you." I shook my head, and told my friend, "Girl, you have your own gift from the Lord."

"I knew you would say that," she said, and we both laughed. Then I admitted that I, too, couldn't help comparing myself to others. For years I'd watched my mother, a great prayer warrior, pray with such eloquent words, strength, and confidence that, whenever I was asked or needed to pray, I unfailingly compared myself to her. I felt intimidated, almost frightened, as if my prayers were not satisfying to God in whatever manner I used to verbalize them.

"You know," I told my friend, "I felt the same way when I was going through that difficult time in my marriage. I came to the office in tears, ready to give up. When you began to pray for me, I said to the Lord, 'Here's another person who prays with great and powerful words, so much better than I.'"

"Really?" my friend asked. "I had no idea!" Then we both laughed again at our silly comparisons.

I couldn't help wondering how often we all seem to err in this regard – comparing ourselves against each other. Some of us take this very human flaw even farther. Instead of dealing with the issue of our own insecurity, we allow the initial feeling of intimidation to birth a seed of jealousy. That seed eventually sprouts bitterness, and flowers into resentment of the other person and his or her special gift.

The Word of God clearly states that we must be satisfied in whatever position we find ourselves (Philippians 4:11): *I am not saying this because I am in need, for I have learned to be content whatever the circumstances.* We need to be content whether we're rich or poor, happy or sad, big-framed or small-framed, a great cook or not, a skilled speaker or not, a bishop or an usher or a congregant who participates with a warm smile from the pew. Although it is sometimes a challenge, I've learned to be satisfied with my own gifts and admire those of others.

I admire my husband's taste in picking home furnishings and other items, when I'd rather buy the least expensive--I can be overly frugal at times! I admire my eldest son's determination to pursue his dreams and my younger son's ability to stick with his own.

I admire my mother's gifts of fervent prayer, wisdom, and teaching, my father's gifts of hospitality and aid to anyone in need, my eldest sister's gifts of understanding and nurture, my younger sister's gifts to encourage and build new acquaintances, my brother's gift of adjusting to new circumstances in a heartbeat, and my Pastor's gift to love and care for those in need.

I admire all the gifts God has placed in my many brothers and sisters – Diana, Tana, Sam, Julio, Courtney, Steve W., Lisa R., Lisa W., Jackie, Angie, Terry, Donna, Vonnie, Bayo, Kelly, Nana, Mom Helen, Pop Marvin, Tom, Art, Onna, Trina, Robin, Vanessa, Teresa, Dave, Trina, Kitten, Chandra, and many more.

But now, I feel confident that "I'm Satisfied with Me."

Simply Follow God's Directions!

It was a brisk, sunny winter's day on January 2, 2007. I sat in my office at work, gospel music playing lightly in the background, as I performed my usual duties at the hospital where I have worked for more than ten years: typing minutes, making meeting arrangements, answering phones, and more. It was just like any other normal day— or so I thought.

As I was concentrating on the tasks at hand, I suddenly heard a simple voice in my spirit say, "Build a website." I paused for a moment and thought, *Build a website? I have no experience in that area. How could I possibly do such a thing?*

Just one day earlier, each of us had welcomed in the New Year in our own way. Some went to a New Year's Eve Watch Night at their local church, some celebrated in their homes, quietly watching the ball drop in New York City via their televisions, and others went to festive social gatherings.

The highly anticipated arrival of 2007 brought a great deal of excitement, with many predictions for this special new year. Why? In part, because of the number seven itself.

In Biblical terms, the number seven has significant meaning. Many call it God's perfect number, and define it as "completion." A quote from Bible Numerics (http://vic.australis.com.au/hazz/Bible Numerics.html) reads: "In the Hebrew, seven ([b'v, - Sheh'-bah) is from a root word meaning to be complete or full. God rested on the seventh day because His work of creation was complete, entire, and perfect. Thus seven represents this perfect completeness and also it represents rest, as in the rest that is taken from work."

Indeed, *(Genesis 2:2-3) reads: "By the seventh day God had finished the work He had been doing; so on the seventh day He rested from all his work. And God blessed the seventh day and made it holy, because on it He rested from all the work of creating that He had done."*

Christians everywhere had looked forward to God blessing their lives this year in great ways: salvation of their loved ones, deliverance from troubling circumstances, launchings of new business ventures, financial blessings, and answers to many other, long-awaited prayers.

I, too, had expected much from The Year 2007. But I had no idea that, just one day into the new calendar, God would send my life in a whole new direction.

I sat there at my desk, trying to focus on my work once again, but I couldn't ignore that insistent voice I had heard. Finally, I typed "website builder" into a search engine on the Internet, and began to do some research. Almost immediately, an entire group of companies offering to help me build a website appeared at my disposal.

Initially, I'd thought that God was telling me to build a website for a ministry of which I was already a member. A few days into my new endeavor, however, I realized that He had another plan in mind for me.

Frustrated and disappointed with the work I had already done—a website template purchased and a flyer typed--I went back to God and asked Him, "Why did You say, "Build a website"? Why would You have me waste my time?"

Right away, God answered. This time, He said, "Build it for the *women's* ministry."

A great sense of relief flooded through me. I remembered how, several years earlier, I'd been told that I would one day be a tool to minister to women of various denominations. Thrilled that this long-awaited vision was finally becoming a reality, a name for the new website sprang to my mind: "Women Regaining Strength."

The name seemed perfect to me. It said everything about the person I had become – a woman nearly broken by certain grave life circumstances who, by God's grace and mercy, regained her inner strength through Christ Jesus. I said, "Lord, this great website name cannot be available; someone must already have it."

Carefully, I typed in the domain name, anxious to see the results. To my surprise and delight, *www.womenregainingstrength.com* was available! Now I knew for sure that God had been speaking to me that day. I immediately purchased the domain and feverishly began building the website, to the best of my abilities.

As the days went by, I kept following God's simple directions, never knowing what was next. Soon, He had given me the complete instructions, and the idea for the first article to be written: "Regaining Strength." He also gave me an editor to make sure the wording and punctuation were accurate, and a few, wonderfully supportive family members and friends who were kind enough to read and critique my new venture when I unveiled it on January 14, 2007.

With $11.95 for a domain name, website builder software from Yahoo Small Business, a computer, an editor, and --most importantly--God's wisdom and instructions, Women Regaining Strength was born.

Now, as I view WRS today--eight months and eight articles later, with new website host Bulletlink, three additional writers, rapidly-growing business and event advertising, and most precious to me, 122 members and counting--I can testify that you don't need a lot of money or a bunch of fanfare to succeed. Though they are often beneficial, you also don't need a long string of educational degrees, nor do you have to be the most computer-savvy person on the planet.

You don't need to know the immediate outcome of your venture-- whether it will be a great success or a disappointing failure-- nor should you focus on the obstacles you might encounter, lest they frighten you off.

All you need is to be willing, with childlike faith, to venture out after hearing God's voice, and demonstrate your obedience to His instructions by your works: (*James 2:26*): *For just as the body without the spirit is dead, so also faith without works is dead.*"

You need to heed His reassuring voice, and "Simply Follow God's Directions!"

My mother, like most mothers, is the historian of the family. Since each of our babyhoods, she's kept photos, awards, and souvenirs of all her children's and grandchildren's ventures and achievements--great and small. The mountain of memorabilia includes heartfelt Mother's Day cards, pictures of my brothers' tours of duty in the Air Force and Army, wedding announcements, prom pictures, photo albums, favorite books, and more.

Every now and then, Mom will remind us kids that, if anything were to happen to the house, such as a fire, a flood, or some other act of God, one of the first things she would try to salvage would be her precious collection of photo albums, with their all-important images, frozen in time.

The other day, while visiting my mother's home to administer her every-six-to-eight-week, touch-up perm, my eldest son called to ask if I would grab a few baby photos for him. Already tired from the eight-hour workday and hoping to go home immediately after completing my mother's perm, I asked him why, in a somewhat annoyed tone. What did he need his baby photos for? My son answered that he wanted to include certain pictures in the photo gallery of his My Space account.

After we hung up, I reluctantly told my mother what her grandson wanted, hoping she would say "no" so I wouldn't have to spend a lot of time going through a barrage of photos. Instead, my mother encouraged me to do so, saying it wouldn't take long for me to get the photos he needed. Her only concern was that my son bring them right back, as soon as he'd made copies.

So, after giving the finishing touches to my mother's hairstyle, I began to flip through all the photo albums she had lodged on top of a shelf in the hallway, a great place to keep them should a very quick exit be necessary. I was still hoping that the task wouldn't be too daunting, and I could grab a few photos in record time. Turning the pages, however, I found myself beginning to relax and enjoy myself as I traveled down the memory lane of our family's history. I found the photos William had requested, placed them to the side, and kept on going.

When I reached a particular page in one of the albums, I began to chuckle. Smack in the middle was a photo of me when I was around 9 years old. No matter how many times my family and I see this photo, we always burst out laughing. Part of the reason for the amusement is because of my unwittingly hideous appearance. I'm sitting on a small, plastic cafeteria chair. In the background you can see the painted, white brick walls of Darley Road Elementary School. My skin looks darker than usual, most likely from the lighting of the black and white photo, and my hair has two very frail-looking plats, one sticking out from each side of the back of my neck. This, undoubtedly, was another of my do-it-yourself hairstyling ventures. I am glad to say that practice eventually made hair-grooming perfect many years later. In my innocent eyes, however, this hairstyle was quite fitting for the time, around 1979. I thought I looked my very best that day, as I sat in great anticipation of a glamorous photo opportunity.

It's a pretty rough-looking portrait of me, all right—and I tell myself that every time I look at it. If ever the validity of the tale of the ugly duckling that eventually became a beautiful swan were in question, this is the proof.

This time, however, I looked more closely at the handwritten sign that I held proudly in my small hands. It read: "Best of the Month." Wow, I thought, as a jumble of memories began to flood back. I suddenly remembered all it had taken to achieve this great honor.

There were at least 250 students at my elementary school, and only nine months in the school year. Each month, one student would be awarded the most prestigious honor in the entire school: "The Best of the Month." This title was held by the honoree for an entire 30 days, along with the prize of some small reward and his or her picture displayed in a glass showcase in the school lobby for all to see.

Now, staring at that old photo, I recalled how shocked and thrilled I was when my teacher informed me that I was the special student chosen for that month. Not just anyone could be the Best of the Month, I remembered. Your grades had to be good, your behavior exceptional, and you could not have been involved in any kind of school detention, suspension, or fight. Being on your best behavior all the time was quite a bit of work, I'd thought at the time.

Later that evening, as I drove home from Mom's house with my son's photos safely tucked beside me, encased in a paper towel and then a plastic bag to ensure their safety on the front seat, I continued to reminisce about the past. I thought of one gorgeous, sunny Sunday as an adult in June 1996, when I made my way to the altar after a morning worship service to rededicate my life to the Lord.

Just a few days earlier, I had been having what I thought was the time of my life, partying with my female friends in a bar. I began to weep now in the car as I continued to drive, thinking of that broken-down person who covered her emptiness and loneliness with stimulants such as alcohol and drugs, which relieved the pain only for brief moments.

Then tears of joy began to flow, and I lifted up my hand to the Lord in a sign of gratitude. For that day at the altar--and for every day forward--I didn't have to be in the best of form. I didn't have to have a perfect record, to never have been in detention, suspended, lost, down-trodden, or broken-hearted. I didn't have to be alcohol, smoke, or foul-mouth free. For God's word in Matthew 11:28 reads: *Come to Me, all you who labor and are heavy laden, and I will give you rest.*

I hadn't been required to come to the Lord with a plan as to how I could change my former self, the woman I had grown into from the little girl who had once been The Best of the Month, for 2 Corinthians 5:17 reads: *What this means is that those who become Christians become new persons. They are not the same anymore, for the old life is gone. A new life has begun!* There was one simple task required of me that day, and that was to simply accept Jesus Christ as my Lord and Savior: Romans 10:9 *For if you confess with your mouth that Jesus is Lord and believe in your heart that God raised him from the dead, you will be saved.*

Someday, I'll take my mother's place as the family historian, and continue our traditions and memories. I now understand more fully the importance of all those precious photos and souvenirs.

As I continued on my journey home, I thought of how every day I do my best, and when I fall short of the mark, the Lord never fails to reward me with His unconditional love and forgiveness. For, in the Lord, each and every one of us is "The Best of the Month."

Don't Miss God's Hand!

It was a Friday at 4:30 p.m., the end of another forty-hour work week. Like most people, my spirit was jubilant as I looked forward to the weekend and two whole days off from the drudgery of work.

There was one stop I needed to make before heading down the highway to the comfort of my home. Every Tuesday, Wednesday, and Friday, our church holds a one-hour prayer meeting, and I planned to attend the service that night.

I dropped by my mother's house to kill the remaining half hour or so before the prayer session began. We sat conversing until the clock read a little after 5:00 p.m., then made our journey together to the church.

Everyone knelt, sat or stood, giving God thanks for another week. We also prayed for the protection and salvation of the lost, and healing for the sick. It was time well spent, we knew, for James 5:16 reads: *The prayers of the righteous avail much.* We left the prayer session feeling refreshed.

I dropped my mother off at her house, and after a kiss, embrace, and good-bye, I started to head home. And that's when I heard it: the most horrible, screeching noise. I rolled down my window and cut the radio to see if the ghastly sound was coming from my car. To my dismay, it was.

As I drove farther down the road, the noise seemed to intensify. The fall evening was warm and sunny, and everyone on their porch steps and at each street corner could hear the dreadful noise, adding to my embarrassment. Didn't I just come from prayer? I asked God. How can You now allow me to go through the headache of having to fix a car, after I just spent an hour praising, worshipping, and giving You glory? Who knew what trouble lurked behind this noise? Surely it will cost me, I thought.

I called my husband to grill him in my frustration: "When you last drove the car, did you hear a noise?" "No," he said. "When you took it in a few weeks ago, they said the brakes looked fine, right?" "Yes," he said. When I insisted that something was wrong and that we needed to fix it right away, he promised to call the mechanic the next day. But tomorrow was too late. I wanted to call someone *right now.* "Well, what about that guy at the church?" my husband asked.

I brightened immediately. Brother Art was well known in our congregation for his mechanical skills and his willingness to help at a moment's notice. After many years of fixing cars, at any time and any place, he had just opened a shop called A & M Auto. He had repaired our car on several occasions, including the time our worn-down battery died right in the grocery store parking lot after Sunday Worship Service one day.

Frantically, I dialed Brother Art's number. He picked up right away and said he was working on another car, but if I gave him an hour he'd meet me at Auto Zone down the street.

Brother Art listened carefully as I pulled the car up. It didn't take much to miss that horrible noise. He assured me that the screeching noise was only an alarm sounding to let me know that the front brakes needed to be done. I felt incredibly blessed that it wasn't something more serious than a needed brake job. That night, Brother Art fixed the brakes in the convenience of my home garage. I was back on the road the very next day, happy that it had been only a minor repair, at an incredibly reasonable cost, and accomplished in record time. What a blessing God had sent our way in Brother Art!

Exactly two weeks later, when I was off from work on another Friday afternoon, I was driving with my eldest son when a construction truck caused a huge rock to hit my windshield. Stunned, I asked my son, "Do you see a crack?" He peered closely at the windshield. "A crack," he said? "No." I felt a huge sense of relief, which lasted just a moment until he added, "Wait a minute. You mean, a crack like that?" Oh Lord, I thought, here we go again. I prayed fervently, Please don't let that crack spread!--to no avail. The crack expanded across the center of the windshield within five minutes. I knew this repair would cost me every bit of $200.00 for a new windshield, and it had to be done right away.

I pulled into our driveway, feeling frustrated once again, and went upstairs to tell my husband the bad news. He offered to start calling around and get some estimates. Leaving my husband to this task, I headed to the basement to start washing clothes. I paused for a moment and asked God, Why? Why is it that when we finally seem to have just a moment of financial stability, another bill comes along? In my despair, I told Him I didn't see the purpose of spending close to $200.00 for yet another repair. How would I now be able to add in an unexpected bill to the budget?

After leaning over the folding table and putting my head down on the pile of clothes to cry for a while, I went back upstairs to my husband. Von had actually found a place that could squeeze us in at 3:00 p.m. that afternoon, at a cost of $175.00. My eldest son said he'd contribute to the finances for the repair. We scheduled the appointment, and by 5:00 p.m. we were leaving the shop with a new windshield-- and I was on my way to another Friday prayer session.

As I knelt to pray, I realized that, in my panic, I had once again missed God's Hand. Not only did God allow the windshield to be fixed immediately, but He had kept us from any danger that could have resulted from a rock hitting our car. I immediately asked God for forgiveness, realizing that I kept missing the ways He always helped me work through difficult situations. When those brakes needed repair, he sent someone to fix them right away, and when the front windshield needed replacement, the finances were somehow in the bank.

So in the busy hustle and bustle of this holiday season, should you find yourself unable to purchase everything you'd like, or if giving a gift to everyone on your list is not possible this year, or if you find yourself unable to give any gift at all, try not to worry. Be thankful that you and your loved ones are alive and well, have a place to lay your heads and food to nourish yourselves, and a loving God who will continue to bless your spirit and supply all of your needs according to His glorious riches in Christ Jesus (Philippians 4:19).

Remember, if things don't always go as planned in your daily life, try not to be consumed by over-concern and stress. Whatever you do: "Don't Miss God's Hand!"

Enjoy a Blessed and Safe Holiday and Remember – JESUS is the Reason for the Season!!

It was December 12, 2007, and I had just sat down to review the past year. I thought about all of the many blessings God had allowed my eyes to see, another faithful, fulfilled year of waiting on His promises, not becoming weary in well-doing, nor prematurely removing myself from the position in which God had placed me. There were many challenges God had carried me through during the past twelve months, and a vast amount of wisdom He had given to allow me to achieve many accomplishments for His Glory, including this website.

It was almost here: January 1, 2008, another highly anticipated year on many Christian calendars. The end of the Year 2007 would signify perfect completion, as according to Bible Numerics, 7 is God's perfect number: Genesis 2:1-3 Reads: *Thus the heavens and the earth were completed in all their vast array. By the seventh day God had finished the work He had been doing; so on the seventh day He rested from all his work. And God blessed the seventh day and made it holy, because on it He rested from all the work of creating that he had done.* Just as the close of this year would bring the end of a cycle and a much-needed rest taken from work, the Year 2008 would soon usher in a new order and the beginning of a new era.

As I continued to reminisce over the soon-to-be-previous year, I remembered that there was one major promise I hadn't fulfilled-- a task I had not completed.

Years earlier, on any given week, you would have found me faithfully heading to the gym to battle the borderline high blood pressure my doctor had warned me about. He'd made it clear that, in order to avoid taking any medications, I would need to exercise regularly and reduce my salt intake.

Almost every day during my lunch hour, I traveled to the eighth floor of the hospital where I was employed to work out in the rehabilitation gym. It was refreshing and invigorating. I could see the benefits of my labor as my blood pressure returned to 120/80, my body became toned, and I felt a great sense of overall accomplishment. I kept up this program off and on for several years, until all the exercising, in combination with a few stressful life circumstances, caused too many pounds to drop from my petite frame. I wasn't happy at the drastic weight loss that had brought my weight down to a size two, so I decided to quit my regular exercise regime.

Some time later, I saw my doctor at the hospital one day as he was visiting another patient. I mentioned my concern regarding the weight loss, and he told me to try eating more. That sounded simple enough, I thought, but as time went on it proved to be a hard task. I found myself barely wanting to eat anything at all as I worried about finances, my job and my marriage. There was only one way to maintain my normal weight, I told myself, and that was to avoid the gym. Weeks turned into months, and soon more than a year had passed without my doing any exercise at all.

After I had reached my normal weight once again, I went for a check-up with my physician. He informed me that my blood pressure was back to the borderline of becoming high again, and made me promise before I left his office that I would resume my exercise program. I agreed, and scheduled a follow-up appointment. A few days later I took out a membership at a local gym, figuring that a new setting would stimulate me. But now, a year and a half later, I had made only a few failed attempts to exercise-- and I had never returned for that follow-up doctor's appointment.

I'd had every intention of keeping the promise I'd made that day to my doctor, of course. But no matter how many times I tried to be consistent with my resolution, I always seemed to fail. Why? Well, I hated to admit it, but the real reason was pretty much a simple case of laziness.

As 2007 drew to a close, I became more conscious of my disobedience to both God and my doctor in not exercising, and I grew increasingly concerned about the promise I had never kept. I decided that in 2008, the Year of New Beginnings, I would make a serious New Year's resolution: a commitment to be faithful to this daunting task of exercise.

The year 2008 has a special significance for Christians. A quote from Bible Numerics (http://vic.australis.com.au/hazz/Bible Numerics. html) reads: "Eight thus represents regeneration and resurrection. When the flood washed the earth clean, in a type of baptism, eight people were saved in the ark. *Which sometime were disobedient, when once the longsuffering of God waited in the days of Noah, while the ark was a preparing, wherein few, that is, eight souls were saved by water (1 Peter 3:20)."* This particular year was the perfect time to start a fresh, new, healthy lifestyle, I thought.

When I shared my thoughts about committing to a better diet and exercise with a friend, she laughed. Many people make false commitments at New Year's, she reminded me. I couldn't argue with her very much on that point, I knew. But I was still determined to change my ways for the benefit of my own well-being.

Later that same week, I discussed my new diet and exercise plans with another friend. He scolded me a bit about my past transgressions and asked, "Why are you going to wait until the New Year? There's no need to put it off any longer. Get started now!" He encouraged me not to try and accomplish everything all at once, but to start off slowly this time, with a few sit-ups here and there. Gradually, he said, you should move up to exercising twice each week, until you're back to working out four to five times a week. I decided to listen to his advice.

The very next day, I signed back up at the gym. On the following Monday, December 17, 2007, I began my new regimen by walking on the treadmill for twenty minutes. The next week I returned to the gym three times, feeling great that I had finally begun to exercise again.

There may be something pressing that each of us failed to complete or do more of in 2007—to study God's Word, pray, fast, worship, start a business or ministry, or enroll in school. Thankfully, we all have another opportunity to start anew in 2008. Let's stay focused together on achieving the goals set before us-- and start a New Beginning!

I'LL TAKE CARE OF THIS

The calendar read December 21st, with only four days left before we would celebrate the birth of our Lord and Savior Jesus Christ. On the agenda for this day--instead of last-minute Christmas shopping and a trip to the supermarket-- was a trip to the veterinarian.

My eldest son, William, brought a dog into our home after his second year at college in Florida. The truth was, I had never wanted a dog, because owning an animal brings so many responsibilities. You have to walk them, bathe them, feed them, and clean up their waste. If you're away from home during the day for any period of time, some dogs like to show their displeasure by chewing on furniture or tearing down decorations. If you plan to take a vacation, you must also plan to send the dog to a kennel, or make other arrangements for its care. And if a dog gets sick, a trip to the veterinarian can prove quite costly.

William—as well as his younger brother-- had always wanted a dog. So when he went away to college and got his own apartment, he also got a dog, despite my objections. And when he came home, he brought his new pet with him. Needless to say, my younger son was delighted, but my husband and I were less than thrilled.

Centaur was the dog's name. Part pit-bull and another unknown breed, he had a beautiful brown coat with hazel eyes-- and a horrible-looking under bite which made him look very mean. But his looks were deceiving, for he was a gentle giant.

Over the next several months, I have to admit that Centaur began to grow on me. He was a great guard dog, always alert at the slightest noise, and good company. My mind still wasn't changed about adding a dog to our household, though. Having been a mom since eighteen, I was now enjoying the increased freedom of having a twenty-year-old and a thirteen- year-old.

Sometime in October, I had noticed Centaur trying to relieve some irritation in his ears. I asked William if he thought the dog had an infection, but my son was sure Centaur just needed his ears cleaned.

56

That didn't seem to work, however, and the irritation grew worse. Now Centaur was in serious discomfort, scratching his ear and shaking his head so much that a vessel burst under his skin, causing a hematoma. The blood bubble was about two inches in length and one inch thick. One ear lay flat and the other protruded outward.

Poor Centaur looked hideous.

When William and I approached the counter at the vet's office, the nurse took one look at the inside of Centaur's ear and informed us that he needed to be seen immediately. The hematoma could burst at any moment and, without an operation, the dog might even bleed to death. My son and I grew increasingly concerned at this frightening news.

I asked the nurse how much we were looking at, cost wise. When I learned that it would be at least a couple of hundred dollars, I told her that we only had one hundred -- and that was William's Christmas money. "Let's see what the doctor can do," she said, and left the room.

While she was gone, I reminded myself once again that this was why I didn't want a dog. I couldn't afford all the money and time it took to care for one. William was very concerned about his little canine friend, whom he treated like his own child. But he had lost his job a couple of months earlier, and had no money to take care of such an enormous bill, either.

We were escorted to Examination Room Two, and in spite of our fears we watched in amusement as Centaur sniffed the entire room, inhaling the scents of previous dog visitors. The nurse came in and took his temperature and gathered some information about his past medical history. William and I then watched a short, informational video about the warning signs of an ear infection, the reasons why certain dogs get them more frequently than others, and how to prevent them. I couldn't help thinking that, if only we had watched this video earlier, we wouldn't be here today facing this huge bill.

The doctor arrived and confirmed that Centaur needed an operation-

-for a grand total of five to six hundred dollars! It was the cheapest rate we would find, she assured us. The particular procedure Centaur required could run up to two *thousand* dollars at another facility.

The vet asked us how much we could pay, and whether we could borrow the rest of the funds, and I said no. William just sat quietly, rubbing Centaur and keeping him calm. I thought of all the other things I could do with five hundred dollars, if I had it, than to pay for a dog's operation. And then I looked at how pitiful the dog looked, and the pain he was in, and I knew that I'd somehow have to get that money for the operation for Centaur.

The good news was that the doctor assured us that the hematoma would not burst, so our pet would not die. The bad news was, it could harden and leave Centaur deformed.

William and I decided to do the best we could for the moment, and pay the $113.00 bill for the appointment and medications to treat the ear infection. As we left the examining room, my son spoke to concerned customers who had inquired about Centaur and commented on what a beautiful dog he was, even with his affliction. But as William tried to keep Centaur calm as other dogs approached, I stood at the counter with my debit card, my worry growing and my heart even more saddened. How or where would we get the money for the procedure Centaur needed? And then I heard the Lord say: *"I'll take care of this."*

Instantly, I felt a huge sense of relief, and my mood lightened. Trusting in God to fulfill His promise, I paid the bill and made a follow-up appointment for Centaur.

On the drive home, William continued to cater to Centaur, who was drooling at the mouth. Oh no, I thought. Centaur is going to get car sick. But William was talking about the possibility of financing the operation, another option the veterinarian had given us. It wasn't available at their center as of yet, but we could shop around at other facilities.

I didn't tell Will what I had heard God speak in my spirit. I didn't want him to become too excited, in case I had heard God wrong. I began to wonder how God would come to our aid. Would He send a lump sum of money? Would He allow us to obtain funds through a financial institution to pay for the operation? Would the veterinarian suddenly offer us a huge discount, or even do the operation for virtually free? How would God accomplish this?

I wasn't entirely sure that I had heard God correctly that day. But I had faith and I knew that was all that was needed. So I waited patiently and anticipated a miracle: *If ye have faith as a grain of mustard seed, ye shall say unto this mountain, Remove hence to yonder place; and it shall remove; and nothing shall be impossible unto you.* (Mathew 17:20)

Soon after we began to give Centaur his medicines, something miraculous indeed began to happen. As each day passed, the hematoma slowly began to disappear. William and I were delighted— and astonished. Then I remembered God's words to me in the vet's office: *"I'll take care of this."*

When we returned to the vet for Centaur's follow-up visit, the nurse who had first greeted us made sure she attended to us. She had been very concerned for Centaur. When she learned that the hematoma had vanished, she was also very surprised. She'd never heard of such a thing happening. I told her that I knew we'd received a miracle.

I also couldn't help but think about the many obstacles we face on a daily basis, and the numerous seeming impossibilities. God's Word states in Mathew 19:26: *Jesus looked at them and said, "With man this is impossible, but with God all things are possible."* And Deuteronomy 28:3 reads: *"Blessed shalt thou be in the city, and blessed shalt thou be in the field."* My mother spoke well when she pointed out that, if God had taken care of our dog, how much more would He do for us? She was certainly right -- everyone and everything in our household is blessed!

So, if you are facing a situation that seems incurable, unsolvable or just plain impossible, rest assured that God is near, saying, "Step aside-- I'll take care of this."

Lord am I in Your Will?

If the day had not been riddled with so many trials and tribulations, I might never have posed the question. But as Fate would have it, May 23, 2007 was the day that everything seemed to go wrong.

That morning, I listened to a voice mail message demanding that we pay a bill immediately or risk being sued. In addition, I learned that our son William would have to come home from college, because we couldn't afford to pay the tuition bill any longer. And then I received the unexpected news that my friend and fellow parishioner Nadine had gone home to be with the Lord. I immediately dissolved into a barrage of emotions and tears.

All of these circumstances shook the core of my foundation-- my faith--and brought to remembrance everything I had been waiting for God to accomplish in my life. I thought of my husband and my hopes for his salvation, and said, "Lord, it's been since July 9, 2004, when you said you'd take care of that, and I'm still waiting." I recalled how God had spoken to me through His servant, a visiting minister, Dr. Long, one Wednesday night about creating a women's ministry and seminar program. God promised me prosperity, ending these days of struggle in my finances. That had been September 9, 2003. I had believed the Lord's words to me that day, and He had promised that the goal of such a ministry would not take more than five to six years to reach fruition. We were now nearing the fifth year.

I thought about college for Will, and how God had supplied the need and allowed him to make it through the first year. I remembered how our church had taken up a collection the next year to pay his first month's tuition. Now, as I sat making arrangements for my son's return home, I felt sorely disappointed. Had sending Will to college been the right thing to do? I questioned the Lord. And if so, why didn't it work out?

I thought about my job, from which I was waiting on God to deliver me. I said, "Lord, you told me that You would deliver me on March 22, 2006. I'm still waiting, and I'm not seeking any new job opportunities.

I've been counting on you to make a way for me to work full-time from home in the ministry one day."

Then I thought about the life-changing month of August 2006, when I'd joined the ministry leadership training program. My pastor had called me out during a service, and told me that it was time for me to prepare for leadership. I was already an instructor for a class of young women and president of the Ministry Of Compassion for the healing of HIV/AIDS. It seemed like a sign from God Himself. Eager to begin, I entered the class at the tail end of another group.

My colleagues before me graduated from the class in April 2007. It was then that I learned I would need to complete my session, and then start over from the beginning with a new group before I could be licensed. I felt extremely disappointed, for in my ignorance I had thought that maybe God would allow me to graduate with the first class. It was not that I had achieved some great feat in class, or arrived at a level where I no longer needed more ministry education, but I was so anxious to be properly licensed as soon as possible to fulfill the Lord's ministry and His Promise. My remaining assignments and training would take at least two more years, well beyond the time frame God had established for my seminars to begin. Was this training program a mistake, too? I wondered.

At work that dismal morning, I began to question all these things, and even my new website ministry Women Regaining Strength. I thought, *I must not be in the Will of God, because nothing is going right.*

I left my desk and took a walk outside to clear my thoughts. That's when I spotted a good friend of mine, one of my brothers in the Lord, and decided to talk to him. He could tell immediately from my expression and my eyes red from crying that something was wrong. When he expressed his concern, I felt another flood of emotions, which spilled into more tears streaming from my eyes. I asked him, "Have you ever reached a point where you were unsure of being in God's Will any longer, when you looked back and thought, Maybe it is me and my self-pride, and not God's Will?" That was exactly the place I was today.

I poured out to my friend all the dilemmas that had made me begin to question my actions. I could live with making mistakes, even though owning up to them was hard at times. But I didn't want to not move on anything God had called me to do, out of fear or lack of faith. Nor did I want to remove myself prematurely from any situation, perhaps just before God's deliverance.

My friend could do little to comfort me that day, other than listen to me vent and pray for me. The answer I needed, he told me, had to come from God Himself.

It was still lunchtime when I returned to my office, so I shut the door and got on my knees to pray. I said, "Lord, I'm not sure if I am in Your Will anymore. Please show me that I can hold on, and endure my trials and struggles a bit longer." Feeling better, but without a definite answer, I got up off my knees and returned to work.

That awful week dragged on, with God fortunately giving me the strength to hold on and wait for His answer. That Sunday, May 27, a guest speaker named Dr. Proctor arrived at our church to deliver a sermon for Youth Day. This was his first time visiting Manna Christian Fellowship, and the first time he had laid eyes on many of us.

Dr. Proctor was a charismatic young man with a witty way of bringing God's Word to our youth, and he repeatedly used his hands and a dramatic tone of voice to emphasize his points. I sat mesmerized in the pew, thoroughly enjoying the Word brought forth that day.

As he concluded his message, he asked all the youth present to come to the front of the church for prayer. He allowed God to speak through him with words of prophecy for many of them. As they stood at the altar, deliverance began to take place in many of them. Several began to cry, and praise God for healing.
Dr. Proctor then moved down the center aisle, praying for some of the adults. As he neared my pew, I began to pray, "Lord, please let this man pass me by. I don't need a personal Word today; I'm just fine with the Word spoken through the sermon." In my heart, I was afraid

something might come to light that I didn't want to hear. Maybe God would even tell me I was out of order. If that were true, it would be a devastating rebuke for me, and something that I would need to reflect upon and find a way to correct.

Dr. Proctor started to walk past me, as if he were moving on toward the back of the congregation. But then he stopped, turned back, and laid his left hand on my forehead with great confidence. Clearly God had something to say directly to me that day. I thought in despair: *Too late, Janice. Here it comes; you were wrong in everything.*

Dr. Proctor told me, "They've been talking about you, but God said, 'Let them talk. I hear the word 'promotion' for you because of your faithfulness.'" When the speaker continued with the words, "You asked if you were in God's Will," a flood of emotions erupted inside me. I remembered the prayer I had sent up just four days earlier. How could this man know my thoughts? *God is speaking to you, Janice,* I realized. I began to cry, knowing that God the Creator of the Universe had decided to stop by that day, and answer an undeserving, sinful servant's plea. Finally, Dr. Proctor finished very sternly, "God says, 'Let this be confirmation that you are in My Will.'"

Now I began to thank God, weeping with uncontrollable joy and gratitude as if I had suddenly received a billion dollars. My tears all but drowned out the latter part of the prophecy: a day when God had also said I would be stress and debt-free.

My girlfriend, who rode home with me that day, asked me in disbelief, "Janice, didn't you hear Him say that also?" I realized that I had not. I had been completely caught up in the knowledge that God had taken the time to answer my prayer. Despite all my recent disappointments, He had wanted to let me know that I was in His Will.

On January 13, 2008--seven and a half months later--God allowed me to receive the promotion He had promised that day. I was licensed into the ministry, and fully prepared for the work to come.

God's Will may sometimes place us in uncomfortable circumstances.

We may feel bound, like Joseph, or humbled before a tormentor, like David. Perhaps, like Jonah, we will be required to return to a job we failed to complete, or even risk our very lives, like Esther.

But whatever the circumstances, we must know that each of us has reassurance from the Lord that all things work together for our good in the end. Trials and tribulations only make us stronger, and more patient.

I hope that my story may help you to hold onto your faith in times of duress, and receive God's strength and encouragement should you one day find yourself asking, "Lord, Am I in Your Will?"

A MOTHER

Mother isn't a word that's flippantly said-it's a word that means hard work, determination, love, strength and dedication, a balancing act every day.

For who else could maneuver such a multitude of tasks-you wash the clothes, prepare the dinner, go to work, school, and theater, create romance with cleverness and pizzazz, and least but not least, draw a child's bubble bath.

You pioneer in everything you do, as single parents, home-makers, doctors, lawyers and educators.

Through your diligence you never seem tire, rest or take a break. (And did someone say retire? Ha!) For even when there's no time, you keep buzzing along like a busy worker bee, the job never-ending for you. Are my clothes pressed, and did you take the dog to the vet? My goodness, you've got so much work to do!

But somehow, to our amazement, you never cease in rising to the occasion, and complete every request without fail. It's no wonder we take this day to salute you and all your ways, and for that we say:

"Happy Mother's Day!"

THE AFTERMATH OF VIOLENCE

There was nothing unusual about the beginning of that day. My son Vaughn and I had our customary morning battle. He tried to stay in bed as long as he could, and I tried relentlessly to get him up and moving. As usual, I went through the ritual of peering into his bedroom, calling, "Time to get up!" And as usual, he ignored my request the first few hundred times.

I couldn't blame Vaughn for prolonging the inevitable. If I had my choice, I wouldn't get up until afternoon, either. I'm not a morning person, and it seems that both of my sons have inherited this trait as well. Finally, deciding that Vaughn had one more chance before I unleashed a storm of fury, I opened the door and saw his bedcovers pulled back and the bathroom door closed. He was up. To ensure he wasn't sleeping on the toilet, I waited for a few seconds until I heard a rush of water from the shower.

After getting dressed, Vaughn and I skipped breakfast and jumped in the car for the thirteen-mile trip into Wilmington. Although we both enjoy a hearty lunch and dinner, neither of us eats in the morning, a habit we need to change as experts say breakfast is the most important meal of the day. We battled through the parade of red tail lights traveling down the busy Route 13 Highway.

"Whose turn is it to pray?" I asked Vaughn. "It's yours, Mom," he quickly responded. *Yeah right,* I thought, but I didn't argue. I said the Morning Prayer.

I dropped Vaughn off at his school, and drove the remaining five minutes to my job.

I pulled up to the garage, swiped my badge and waited as the lever rose, granting my car entrance. After parking, I walked briskly to the Corporate Services building, swiped in at the Kronos timeclock reader, and took the elevator to my fifth floor office.

I already knew that this day would most likely be a busy one. The hospital's insurance policy was ending soon, and we were signing up with a new carrier. That meant any hospital incidents with the possibility of turning into a lawsuit needed to be reported. I had about 30 letters to compose after reviewing the case histories. My co-worker Debbie faced a similar daunting task. Neither of us spent much time talking that day. We worked feverishly to complete the jobs ahead of us.

I could hear the traffic outside, whisking over the four-lane bridge off the Washington Street Extension. Underneath, with the Brandywine River no longer raging from the invasion of melting snow and ice, the water flowed peacefully down its murky river banks.

The weather forecast was for a whopping 70 degrees. Pet owners and nature-loving cyclists and runners were enjoying the walking trails along the river, taking in a refreshing reprieve from chilly weather.

From my window I could see the treetops, still unclothed in their green glory, the bark of their branches resembling a rich brown soil.

The sun made its presence known with such a warm intensity that it might have fooled a newly-dubbed Delawarean into believing the days of 30 to 40 degree weather were over. But I knew well that spring on the East Coast is full of uncertainty. By tomorrow, I could be watching a snow flurry outside this very same window.

Debbie's radio was blasting and I could hear the theme music for the Channel 6 Action News. It had to be 12 p.m. Faithfully at each day around this time, my colleague would increase the volume on her radio to listen to the mid-day broadcast.

My own radio played softly in the background, tuned to my favorite gospel radio station: Praise 103.9. It was almost time to take a break. By now I was starting to feel hunger pains from not eating all day.

I continued to work for a few more minutes, hoping to put one more dent in my work load. That's when I heard a loud commotion outside my window. Startled and curious, I cut down my radio to see if I could figure out who or what was causing the clamor. Arguments outside the hospital were nothing unusual, due to its location right in the heart of the city. Most disagreements were resolved quickly and amicably, without the need for security or police intervention.

I turned my attention back to my work, only to hear the squabble arise once again. This time the urgency of the voices had intensified. "No, no, don't do it, man," I heard one say, followed by a: *Pop, pop, pop, pop, pop.*

Frantically I jumped up, whisked my chair to the side, and rushed to the window. Raising the blinds as high as they would go, I braced myself in the center of the window and leaned closer until my lips were almost kissing the glass. My eyes immediately locked onto a group of young men below, who were now hiding behind parked cars in a lot across the street.

My heart began to race with anxiety as I tried to understand what was going on. Then I saw another young man in a white shirt and blue jeans, standing half in the street and half on the sidewalk. A gray bicycle lay next to him on the ground. The young man had his arm extended straightway between his chest and upper body, as if he were reaching for something. There were no more words exchanged between him and the other young men, still crouched behind the cars.

The sun shone so brightly at that instant that its glare bounced off an object that graced his hand, making it impossible to identify. A few moments later, the glare dissipated, clearly revealing the object.

It was a gun.

Shocked and horrified, I continued to watch as all the young men began scurrying in different directions. The one in the white shirt ran down the street—hurriedly at first, as if he were in a 100-yard dash. Then, just as quickly as he had begun his sprint, he slowed as if he were somehow losing his zeal, or making a feeble attempt to catch his breath. His run decelerated to a sluggish trot and then a skip, mimicking an intoxicated adult playing a game of hop-scotch. Then his body began a downward spiral to the black pavement below.

Repulsed and terrified by the scene I had just witnessed, I screamed for my co-worker: "Debbie, Debbie did you see that?"

My colleague was mum. In a panic, I yelled, "Oh my God! Someone got shot!" Trembling with fear, I ran from my office to the elevator a few feet away, and back to my office, not knowing what to do. There was no hospital protocol for a catastrophe such as this.

Debbie hurried down the hall to check on everyone else. I went back to my office, still feeling stunned. I wanted to cry, but I couldn't—my emotions seemed frozen.

I returned to the window and gazed down the street. *Maybe he's okay,* I thought.

But the young man lay motionless on the pavement below. People began to gather near his crumpled body.

What should I do? I asked myself, for in my panic it escaped me to pray. I had watched plenty of movies with gun battles and horror flicks. Why was I now at a loss as to a course of action? But this was not a movie, with fake blood, people eluding a barrage of bullets, and the hero running off into the sunset with his lover, unscathed. This was real, and below lay a young man battling for his life in the aftermath of violence.

Employees from other parts of the building began flooding to our floor in frenzy. No one knew if the other perpetrators were inside the hospital or not. Security personnel came to check on our safety. I continued to watch out my window as sirens screamed and police officers began to swarm the crime scene, blocking off the streets.

Across the street, people began streaming out of a nearby building, and soon after, an ambulance arrived. *Thank God,* I thought. A few moments went by, as emergency technicians worked feverishly on the young man. I began praying that God would somehow spare his life. The emergency technicians continued their efforts for what seemed like an eternity. Finally, they rose and stepped away, equipment in hand. *What are they doing?* I thought. *Why aren't they placing him on a stretcher and rushing him to our emergency room only a few yards away?* A moment later I received my answer, as a white sheet dancing rhythmically in the slight breeze found its resting place over the young man's lifeless body.

"Oh, my God!" I cried, in agony. "He's gone; he's gone!"

For the rest of the day, I sat at my desk, trying to work, but feeling completely comatose. Periodically I rose to the window to see what was happening outside. At one point I heard the now massive crowd gathered on the street screech in horror. Later I learned that part of the sheet covering the young man's body had flipped back in the wind, for a moment revealing his corpse.

Police officers directed the crowd to move back as a black coroner's van made its entrance and parked a few yards from the body. It took hours to rcmovc the young man and evaluate the crime scene, which extended two blocks from the discharged gun shells and incorporated a few parked cars riddled with bullets. I thanked God that no one else had apparently been harmed.

I managed to make it home that evening, playing and replaying the events I had witnessed over and over in my head like a broken record. I thought about my two sons, twelve-year-old Vaughn, and William, who was away at college and nineteen years old, the same age as the young man who had lost his life. I talked with them both that evening about the importance of making wise decisions in the company they keep, and about being careful of the areas they frequent. Once again, I reinforced my stance on their never picking up or being around anyone with a gun. I was grateful to God for keeping them both safe.

After a few days of continued shock, life began to return to some normalcy, but I knew I could never erase the memory of this incident. Like the inscription on a concrete monument, it had etched its place in the corridors of my mind forever.

Today was April 9, 2008, just one day away from the second anniversary of that horrific event. Debbie stopped in my office to remind me of the date. "I know," I told her, "I was thinking about it the other day." She asked whether there was a shrine at the bus stop, the place nearest to where the young man had taken his final breath. There wasn't, I knew—I had checked in the morning as I was coming into work.

It was amazing to me that we both still recalled that day so vividly that we didn't even need a calendar marking the date, or a computer-generated reminder. Instinctively, we remember.

During my lunch hour, I thought about the young life taken too soon, and the many lives lost daily due to senseless violence.

I thought about robberies committed for dollars, murders for gang initiations, and innocent children caught in the crossfire of bullets from drug dealings gone wrong. I recalled officers who had sworn to uphold the peace and protect those unable to protect themselves, gunned down for no reason. I thought about suicide bombers and terrorist attacks and the people left hurting in their wake.

Then I thought about the wives, husbands, children, siblings, mothers, fathers and friends, all grieving over lives lost to violence. I thought about the memorials and vigils held in remembrance of their loved ones, and the emotional, economic and health effects of these tragic circumstances.

My grief was just a small part of how they, the victims in the aftermath of violence, must feel: healing but never forgetting.

I wonder whether many of the perpetrators of violence would change their decision to pick up a gun if they knew that the end result would cost them their lives. I wonder if they would regret their actions if they knew that a stray bullet had ended the future of a bright-eyed six-year-old whose only crime had been to be in the wrong spot at the wrong time. Or if, after peering into a bedroom at night and seeing a wife or husband still clinging onto any piece of clothing that might release the scent of a lost loved one, or witnessing mothers and fathers burying their own children, they would stop and rethink their behavior.

I wonder if any of those young men on that fateful day would have stopped if they knew: The Aftermath of Violence.

The clock on my computer screen read 4:38 p.m. It was finally time to clock out from work and head home.

A quick shutdown of the computer, with the Windows log-out theme playing cheerfully to let me know the task was near completion, and I was on my way. *Don't forget to leave your door unlocked, Janice,* I reminded myself. John, the man who cleans our office, would be vacuuming our floors tonight.

"Good night, Lisa!" I called to my co-worker, and waited patiently for the elevator to arrive. I punched out on the Kronos time clock at 4:41 p.m. and headed toward the parking garage.

The sky had been overcast with sleep-inducing clouds and rain for most of the day. Earlier I had fought to stay awake at my desk, but now the sunshine was peering through, warming and brightening the end of my workday.

As I walked to my car, I began a quick prayer, asking God to help me through the rest of the day. Then I went over all the things I needed to do that night. *Okay,* I told myself, *You have to pick up Will from work, then stop by the grocery store to get a few items for dinner—you're cooking cheeseburger subs. You have to be home in time for Little Von's haircut appointment, and wash a load of clothes. And later, if you have time, you'll need to get on the computer and work on this month's WRS issue.* My walk became brisker as I reviewed the long list of agenda items. There was no time to waste.

I climbed the two flights of stairs leading to the parking level where I had left my car, and turned the handle on the orange painted door. But just as I spotted the back of my black Nissan Altima parked at the top of the incline, I heard someone say, "Excuse me, can you help me?"

Immediately I thought, *What now? Who dares to interrupt my busy schedule to add still another item?* At that moment, I was surely not displaying the character of Christ.

I gathered myself and turned with a smile, hoping that whatever this person wanted would not take long. There stood a petite, middle-aged woman with long blonde hair, wearing black pants and a bright pink shirt. She could not have weighed more than a hundred pounds. In her right hand she grasped a gray and black cane, which she was clearly using to balance herself. The expression on her face was one of distress and worry. In spite of this, I again wondered what she might demand that would delay my long-anticipated departure from work. "Sure," I said, trying to be polite. "What do you need?"

"I've been walking around this garage for an hour," the woman said, her voice trembling slightly, "and I can't find my car." She looked as if she were about to cry. I gazed at her cane and impaired leg and thought of how tough it must have been for her, walking around the five-floor, bi-level parking garage. She must be tired now, and at her wit's end.

"Of course," I told her. "I'll call our Security Department. They can ride you around in our company van and help you find your car." I would have offered to drive the woman myself, but I knew that inviting a stranger into one's car, even a tiny, polite, disabled woman, was not safe these days. I decided to follow the protocol of our hospital, and made the call. A young man answered, and told me that someone would be right there.

As we waited for the van, the woman confided in me how mortified she was that she could not find her car. "There's no need to be embarrassed," I told her. "I've lost my own car in this garage on quite a few occasions, and I work here." This seemed to reassure the woman a bit, and we both laughed.

When I mentioned that I was on my way to pick my son up from work, the woman told me that she would be fine, and insisted that I go ahead. Reluctantly, I agreed, but I wrote down the numbers for the Security Department and the hospital operator for her, just in case. As I finished the note, I saw the hospital security van pull around the corner outside on the street. I decided to wait a little while longer, figuring that it would reach us very soon.

A few minutes later, there no further sign of the security van. "Please go," the woman urged. "I don't want you to be late to pick up your son." But by then my Godly character and sense of moral duty had kicked in, and I told her that I would stay. I knew it was more important that I made sure she was safe.

More time passed without the arrival of Security, and I began to wonder if they had gotten lost. I looked around the garage and over the concrete divider, but still the van did not appear. The woman once again told me that she'd be fine, but I knew she was just being nice, and would no doubt feel more comfortable if I stayed. I assured her that I wouldn't leave her, and was rewarded by the look of great relief on her face.

At long last, the van came around the corner and down the incline. I helped the woman into her seat, and asked the security officer to take good care of her. She thanked me with a warm smile as I shut the door behind her. Her nightmare was over.

I rushed to my car and looked at the time: 4:51 p.m. Not bad at all, I thought. I wouldn't be very late to pick up Will. I quickly put on my seatbelt, adjusted the radio, and proceeded down to the next level of the parking garage. To my amazement, the security van was slowing to a stop on the bi-level above me. The passenger door opened and the woman emerged, with a wave and a big smile on her face. She had finally found her car-- just one level up from where she had been searching!

I remembered my initial reaction to the woman's request for help, and how far it had been from the example Jesus left for all of us to help one another. Now I thanked God for interrupting my busy day.

As I rode home I noticed that the traffic was incredibly light, as if God were rewarding my act of helping another. I arrived at Will's place of employment at exactly 5:05 p.m. The Lord had not allowed me to be even one minute late!

God's Word resonated in my spirit: (Acts 20:35): *In everything I did, I showed you that by this kind of hard work we must help the weak, remembering the words the Lord Jesus himself said: "It is more blessed to give than to receive."* (2 Corinthians 9:2): *For I know your eagerness to help, and I have been boasting about it to the Macedonians, telling them that since last year you in Achaia were ready to give; and your enthusiasm has stirred most of them to action.*

I thought about ways in which each of us could be more helpful to others--with a prayer, a word of encouragement, a listening ear. Many of us could donate time to worthy organizations and causes, or monetary funds to missions against violence, programs for substance abuse awareness, and research grants toward the cure of illnesses such as cancer, HIV/AIDS, and diabetes, to name a few. We could also sponsor educational grants and enable those in other countries to acquire necessities such as clean water, medicines, and other aids.

The possibilities seem endless for us to help one another daily, no matter how limited our funds, time, or patience. Through our own actions, we can all play an important role in stirring others to answer the desperate call: "Can You Help Me?"

It was the end of September 2006 and the kids were back to the hustle and grind of the school year. I had already begun to miss the summer months. *How had they passed so soon?* I wondered. It seemed like only yesterday that the children were running around playing without a care in the world—no homework, no classes, just enjoying their summer vacation. And I had enjoyed it as well. I didn't have to come home every night and ask the kids if they had homework. I wasn't required to look over a slew of misspellings in my youngest son's papers after his attempt to finish his work quickly so he could go outside and play. *Why did those restful months have to end?* I asked myself.

As I headed home from work, I noticed that the traffic was back to its usual heavy volume, with the additional flow of school buses and cars filled with people no longer taking long weekends at the beach. The usual twenty-five minute drive turned into forty minutes, but I waited patiently. There was no need to complain. After five years, I was quite used to this ritual of early fall.

I pulled into my housing development, anticipating a restful night at home with my family. But to my amazement as I turned the corner, I saw my husband's gray Chevy Impala parked in the driveway. It was an unusual event for Von to be home before me, as he normally made a couple of stops to friends' houses or a lounge after work to watch a ball game.

I was also used to being the first one home as several years earlier Von had worked the nightshift at the auto assembly plant. For a time, I had almost felt like a single parent. Von and I used our Saturdays and Sundays well during those years, since weekends were the only real times we saw each other.

I hit the garage door opener, parked my car, and headed to our mailbox, which stood at the bottom of the driveway. The street was abuzz with kids playing a game of basketball with a stand-alone court next door. The cold weather had not yet hit us with its fierceness and so we were all still enjoying summerlike temperatures. I reached into the mailbox and pulled out a few pieces of junk mail. *Don't they ever get tired of sending this stuff?* I thought. Among the mail was a white 12 x 9 envelope with McCuller and Frentz, a law firm, as the return address. *More junk mail,* I told myself. I could open it later.

I made my way to the house and turned the knob on the black door. I walked through the living room and past the kitchen to the family room, where Von sat watching ESPN. My husband could watch those highlights all night long and never tire of them. I hoped he would move to the TV upstairs soon because I wanted to listen to my nightly news as I prepared dinner. Luckily, he usually moved without a hassle. "Hey," he said now, in his usual way of greeting me. "Hey," I replied, tossing the mail on the coffee table. "Not much today. Just some junk mail and a letter from someplace called McCuller and Frentz." "Open it up," he said, with a shrug. I tore away at the envelope and pulled out a quarter-inch package of papers. *What is this?* I thought. It looked serious–like some kind of court notice. I was very familiar with the look of court papers, having worked as a legal secretary for years.

I stood for a moment, no doubt with a look of terror on my face. Von must have noticed because he immediately stopped watching the action on the TV screen. "Janice, what is it?" he asked. I didn't answer, as I was too busy reading. The heading of the document read: "Notice Of Motion Of Mortgage Electronic Registration Systems, Inc. For Relief From Stay Under 11 U.S.C. Section362(d) (1) For Lack Of Adequate Protection."

"What is it?" Von asked again, more sternly this time. He was sitting up now, his feet planted firmly on the floor as he leaned forward on the edge of the couch, awaiting my response. "A lawsuit," I answered, feeling stunned. "From the mortgage company." I flipped through the barrage of documents in despair. It looked as if they were asking the court for permission to sell the house. Von let out a deep sigh and placed his hand to his forehead as he dropped his head – his usual reaction when stressed. He looked as shocked as I felt. I continued to scan the papers as my husband sat silently staring at me from the couch. I could see the worry in his eyes.

Another wave of panic set over me as I frantically flipped through the pages once again. There were the terms of our mortgage: $153,050.00, 30 years, 7.375% interest, mortgage began October 1, 2001, present monthly mortgage payment of $1,183.69. But the attached Exhibit A listed late payments of $3,551.07. *What?* We had just sent off one payment and were about to double up with two more payments in the upcoming week. But now, it seemed, it was too late to catch up. Then I saw that late charges of another $84.56 had been added, for a grand total of $3,634.63. I gasped. How were we going to get out of this dilemma? We had many bills coming up and there was no way, with Von's income and mine, that we could pay such a large lump sum. Exhibit C listed all of our payments to date since we had filed for bankruptcy in August 2005. The headline of Exhibit D said: "Mark America Default Services Inc." followed by, to my horror, a 4-page appraisal of our home. The first page gave specifications of the house: Colonial, Semi-detached, 1,520 square footage, 6 rooms, 3 bedrooms, 2.5 baths, .20 acre lot, 100% basement, 2 Car Attached Garage, Age 3 years. I read on, Probable sales price 265,000; suggested list price 267,000; 30 Day Quick Sale 260,000; Subject Land Value 60,000. They even listed sales prices of comparable homes that had sold in our area over the last two years. I was even more upset when I saw photos of our home and our street. How did they get those pictures? Later I found out that the bank had hired an independent appraiser who walked around outside our home one day and took photographs.

I let out a sigh and sat down next to Von on the couch. My husband looked defeated. It did seem hopeless that we could ever get out of this situation. I felt a sense of fear come over me like never before. My hands were glued to the papers as I handed them over to Von and then waited in silence as he read them.

Von and I had mismanaged our money for years. We were always struggling to keep our home. It wasn't easy taking on a mortgage and all the additional expenses that went along with buying a home: the water bill, sewage, maintenance, etc.— things we didn't have to worry about when we were renting. Finally, we had elected to file Chapter 13 Bankruptcy to relieve the strain of financial hardship. It was a hard decision that we fought to the bitter end, but it was the only choice we had to keep the home for which we had labored for so long. But even after the courts approved the payment schedule to our debtors, we had still ended up behind on our bills.

I knew I had been partly to blame for where we were financially. I had done all I could to correct the situation-- tightening the budget, scrimping on purchases like clothes and household items--but it still wasn't enough.

We had already exhausted every area for relief from our financial woes. *Janice, there's nothing you can do right now,* I told myself. I looked around at our house, with all its fond memories. I thought about my children and how much they would miss living here, and all the friendships they had formed in the neighborhood. I thought about the two-bedroom apartment we had lived in for many years until we had outgrown it and made the decision to purchase a house. I remembered the months of searching for exactly the home we wanted. I even recalled watching the foundation being poured for our new house and all the days we had driven by, taking pictures of the shell before it became the sanctuary we dwelled in today.

How I would miss this place, but what more could I do? Only God could deliver us from this dilemma now. I knew that I was going to have to make a choice. Either I could worry myself to death over something I couldn't change, or I could trust in God and choose to make peace with this situation. *Which is it going to be?* I asked myself.

I chose peace: the peace that only God could provide and that surpassed all understanding. The instant I made that decision, I felt a sense of peace and contentment.

Silently, I rose from the couch, leaving Von, who didn't understand my trust in God, to peruse the documents. My husband didn't know that I had recalled a promise the Lord had made me long ago—that because of my faithfulness to Him and to my marriage, we wouldn't lose anything. Though we had faced many legal and financial battles that put us on the brink of foreclosure, repossession, lawsuits, and judgments, God always kept that promise. And even if I had heard

God wrong all those years ago, there was nothing I alone could change about the situation—there were no "do-overs" for our problem.

A half hour passed after Von and I had learned of our current dilemma. I headed toward my bedroom to pray, since it's still early, resolving again in my spirit that I wasn't going to worry about this situation tonight. Besides, I told myself, our house was only a material possession. I was already blessed with my health, my family, a job, and the peace that God had given me, which was beyond comprehension.

In the following days my husband and I spoke with our lawyer, who had also received the lawsuit papers. She told us that we still had options and I immediately began to thank God. Our lawyer would put in a motion to the court to place us on a repayment plan for the back months and reduce the $1,000.00 monthly Chapter 13 payments we were making to pay back our debtors in addition to the mortgage payment. The reduction in payments helped Von and I to maintain our budget and keep our house.

Over the next tough six months, we paid the outstanding $1,183.69 for the current mortgage plus an additional $600.00 for court fees and the late mortgage payments. We had to tighten up on our finances even more, but we made our payments faithfully.

Now, a little more than two years later, every time I pull up to our two-story colonial house and park in our two-car garage and go to our mailbox to retrieve the mail, I'm thankful. Von and I have only three more months of payments left until our bankruptcy will be discharged. God kept His promise and we are still here in our home. Nothing was lost.

There comes a point in each of our lives when we have to make a choice: We can allow the stress of devastating circumstances, such as divorce, financial disaster, or loss of a home, job, car or loved one sicken us with worry. Or we can trust in God and find a place of peace and contentment in situations we can't change. For what amount of worry can change anything? Matthew 6:27-34 reads: *Who of you by worrying can add a single hour to his life? And why do you worry about clothes? See how the lilies of the field grow. They do not labor or spin. Yet I tell you that not even Solomon in all his splendor was dressed like one of these. If that is how God clothes the grass of the field, which is here today and tomorrow is thrown into the fire, will he not much more clothe you, O you of little faith? So do not worry, saying, 'What shall we eat?' or 'What shall we drink?' or 'What shall we wear?' For the pagans run after all these things, and your heavenly Father knows that you need them. But seek first His kingdom and his righteousness, and all these things will be given to you as well. Therefore do not worry about tomorrow, for tomorrow will worry about itself. Each day has enough trouble of its own.*

As I look back now on that devastating day, I'm so thankful that I Chose Peace.

Women Regaining Strength Christian Magazine

You're invited to join WRS and the message of encouragement,
strength and hope in Jesus Christ.

Visit www.womenregainingstrength.com to find FREE valuable
resources of inspiration.

Or write us at:

Women Regaining Strength Publishing Company, LLC
P O Box 11583
Wilmington, Delaware 19850

WRS

To God Be The Glory!